RAP AND THE EROTICIZING
OF BLACK YOUTH

MICHAEL PORTER

Chicago, Illinois

First Edition, First Printing

Front cover illustration by Harold Carr

Copyright © 2006 by Michael Porter

All rights reserved.

Printed in the United States of America

10-Digit ISBN #: 1-934155-02-0
13-Digit ISBN #: 9 781934 155028

CONTENTS

Introduction   iv

1. The Child Erotic   1

2. The Hijacking of Children's Sexual
   Development   11

3. Does BET Stand for "Black Eroticizing
   Television"?   19

4. Tweening   29

5. Sexualized America   37

6. When Pathology Becomes a Norm:
   Hip-Hopping into Madness   47

7. Does Your Daughter Want To Be a
   "Video Ho"?   57

8. Player or Sexual Predator?   65

9. How Rappers Are Being Pimped   71

10. Where Y'all At?: Positive Rappers
    Search for a Black Audience   79

11. Rap and Manhood Development   91

12. Rap and Womanhood Development   99

13. Recommendations   103

Endnotes   115

"I wrote these words for everyone

Who struggles in their youth,

Who won't accept deception

Instead of what is truth.

It seems we lose the game

Before we even start to play.

Who made these rules? We're so confused,

Easily led astray"

—Lauryn Hill, from her song, *Everything is*

Everything

"What happened to the dreams of a girl president?

She's dancing in the video next to 50 Cent."

—Pink, from her song, *Stupid Girls*

Introduction

Black boys and girls are eroticized through their exposure to negative Rap lyrics and videos. Their sexual development is being hijacked, and we must save them. This book is written in the belief that in order to save Black children, and consequently Black people, we must take a critical look at the mental diet fed to Black children. The mental diet does not only consist of academic curriculums, which in the case of the Black child are often miseducational, but also includes the musical lyrics and music-related images that go into the minds of children and adolescents. As you are aware, the consumption of healthy food develops a healthy body. The eating of unhealthy foods leads to an unhealthy body, consequent illness, and sometimes death.

When positive, life-enhancing images and messages/information are fed into a child's mind, the result is a mentally and emotionally balanced, healthy child. Likewise, when negative messages and negative images are fed into a child's mind, the child becomes sick and will reveal destructive beliefs and values, an unhealthy self-image, and dangerous behaviors. Too many Rap songs and Rap videos feed unhealthy messages and unhealthy images into the minds of Black children and are, as a result, destructive to Black children.

If it takes an entire village to raise one Black child, then it is necessary that Black adults identify threats to successfully raising conscious, competent, and physically, mentally, and spiritually healthy Black children. If the unprotected child becomes a messed up child, he or she is likely to become a messed up adult. This messed up adult will probably bring children into the world, thus assisting in implementing and maintaining a cycle of dysfunctional, destructive beliefs and behaviors in the village. A Black child's mental diet of negative Rap songs, negative Rap videos, and negative Rap personalities serves to further disrupt our already overburdened and greatly troubled Black village.

Before going further, let me state right now that I am not addressing the rejoinder, "Well, what about White children? They listen to Rap, too, and buy lots of Rap music." White society utilizes a socioeconomic safety net for Whites that is not available to prevent Black folks from falling to destruction.

If the popular White Rapper, Eminem, decided to stop rapping and began to speak properly and behave in a decent manner, he would have no problem or obstacles in meeting his non-Rapper goals in American society. Sean Combs could not do the same because he would encounter what Black men encounter daily: Racism. Therefore, I am unapologetically addressing the destructive effects of negative Rap songs, negative Rap videos, and negative Rap personalities on Black children, with particular emphasis on negative Rap influences on child and adolescent sexual views, desires, and behaviors. Now let's continue.

Introduction

Pathology refers to illness. It is pathological to write, produce, and provide air time to songs and videos that use such words as "b*****s," "hos," "motherf*****s," "niggers," "f***," "dogs," "freaks," and "thugs" and encourages and glorifies killing and sexual promiscuity. It is pathological to target Rap videos that resemble soft porn to children and adolescents. Understand that if something pathological is done often enough, and mostly goes unchallenged, it is given social approval via default on the part of the Black community/village, spreads like wildfire, and would even have its victims scratching their heads trying to figure out what is wrong with their children and their community even as they continue to engage in these widely accepted pathological behaviors. In other words, a person and a people can be crazy as hell and not know it. They will even begin to delight in their craziness. This craziness then becomes an established way of life and even a highly profitable industry.

Again, Black boys and girls are eroticized through their exposure to negative Rap music and videos. This means that their sexuality is being manipulated and strongly influenced by the lyrics, video images, and personalities of the Rap industry—and it is an industry. This eroticizing of Black children is a strong threat to Black people, and hence a strong threat to the village. Some say this is artistic creativity. I disagree. Is it artistic creativity to call Black females b*****s and hos (and for some females to proudly call themselves b*****s and hos) while graphically describing how you will f*** them and, generally, disrespect them? No, this is not artistic creativity; this is pathology.

With all the madness in the Black community, we do not have the luxury of skirting around this reality. If we have to "hate" on some of this pathology, then so be it. It matters not that we like some of the men and women who Rap. Just as you may have to punish a child you love for the purpose of teaching them a healthy way of living and interacting with others, we must do the same with those Rappers we like but who carry negative messages that lead to a range of inappropriate behaviors by their young fans, who are our children and grandchildren.

Understand: We cannot discuss AIDS in the Black community and not discuss the sexual influence of too many Rap songs and videos. We cannot discuss teen pregnancy in the Black community and not discuss the sexual influence on our children and adolescents of too many negative Rap songs and videos. We cannot discuss adolescent sex offenders in the Black community without discussing the sexual influence of negative Rap songs and videos (especially the videos). Also, we absolutely cannot afford to hold any discussion whatsoever about murder, drug dealing, and drug use in the Black community without discussing the negative influence of too many Rap songs, performers, and their accompanying videos. We are only fooling ourselves if we think that there is no need to examine how negative Rap songs and negative Rap videos impact our youths' beliefs and behaviors for the worse.

Though it is a fact that a wicked combination of miseducation and racism has given rise to Black poverty, crime, and other destructive behaviors and conditions which seek to keep Blacks in subservient positions, we must *still* confront the negative influence of too many Rap songs and videos. That a young Brother would state "Sh**, man, a niggah writin' what he sees and writin' about how that sh** make him feel!" does not justify him unintentionally influencing other young Brothers and Sisters to destroy themselves.

If these types of Rap songs and videos had the "snake serum" effect, they would be a blessing to the Black community. When a snake bites you, the physician gives you medicine derived from a snake to cure you. If Rap songs brought about a *decrease* in the madness inflicting Black communities, our condition would change almost overnight. But, Brothers and Sisters, when Snoop Dogg calls himself a gangster and a Crip and then calls Black females b*****s and hos, he is not encouraging 13, 14, 15, and 16-year-old Black males to refrain from calling Black girls b*****s and hos or to refrain from killing each other. He is encouraging them to do such things, and to do them with a vengeance. Though his and others' negative influence may be unintentional, it is very destructive and must be confronted if lives are to be saved.

In general, American media and popular culture are the catalysts for all the madness stated above. Blacks live under an umbrella of White media/corporate influence on our minds and emotions from cradle to grave. Rappers are really being pimped by a system that historically and presently exploits, degrades, and destroys Black people. The fact that a young Black male would diligently work toward becoming his mind's fantasy-come-to-life Mafia gangster; a pimp; or a criminal (thug) is what Amos N. Wilson calls a "social creation." (Wilson, 1993)

Jawanza Kunjufu wrote an excellent book entitled *Hip-Hop vs. MAAT: A Psycho/Social Analysis of Values*. He stated of this ancient African concept and lifestyle, that "MAAT is expressed in the seven cardinal virtues of righteousness, truth, justice, harmony, balance, reciprocity, and order. MAAT is the right way, or path, of righteousness." Kunjufu's title is timely because negative Rappers are in a heavyweight fight with MAAT (fortunately, Kunjufu has recently written *Hip Hop Street Curriculum: Keeping It Real*). All or most negative Rappers are self-destructive; whenever a person deliberately goes against truth, justice, and righteousness, that person is hell bound and, thereby, self-destructive.

We must take back our children. We must rescue them and simultaneously teach them to identify danger and to save themselves. "We" is the key word here; the village is "us" and "we" are the village. Now come on and let's go rescue our children!

"Isn't it ironic how erotic it is to watch 'em in thongs."
—50 Cent, from his song, *Candy Shop*

1. The Child Erotic

You see it in elementary, middle, and high schools. You see it in your neighborhood. You see it in grocery stores and at gas stations. You see it in your home. Girls, ages 8, 9, 10, 11, 12, 13, and older dressed in tight and revealing fashions. Thong straps revealed above their jeans, with just enough buttocks showing to provoke male desire; sometimes accentuated with a tattoo on the small of the back. Navel revealed, often with a ring attached. Walk is mildly to ridiculously exaggerated, as if vying for someone's attention. These girls make an effort to appear mature, and some of them even use vulgar language, thus making certain they are looked at and perceived as mature or "down." Even when their eyes reveal uncertainty and unease about their bodies and how they are dressed, the social pressure compels them to continue.

These girls are mostly uncomfortable with their bodies and with revealing their bodies but have learned from videos, songs, movies, and the way boys (and men, too) approach them that it is their bodies that have attracted male attention and praise. From childhood, these Black girls have witnessed music videos; male and female family members, Black sitcoms on television, and their favorite Rappers praise the Black female's behind, often in the most derogatory terms. These young girls become vulnerable because their normal desire to be liked and appreciated is misconstrued and subsequently exploited. They unknowingly become the socially created victim better known in popular culture (Rap jargon) as "bait," "ho," "b****," "freak," "hood rat," "chicken head," "skeezer," and "dime." And, sadly, many of these young Black girls will grow to love being called these derogatory names. Black folk, we have a real mess ahead of us!

Some of these girls have been told by their equally mis-socialized mothers that, "My baby gonna get all them boys liking her. She cute and got a shape already!" The parent then dresses their girl-child like Lil Kim. This girl is receiving a very strong message that her body is the most important thing about her. At home she is dancing to a variety of Rap songs and videos, including the most vulgar, sexually provocative songs and videos. She begins to mimic the gestures, dance, and social interaction style of older girls, the video dancers, and adult women. Boys give her attention, and her belief that her body is all she is becomes strengthened in proportion to this increase in male attention. This girl is learning that using her body is the way to form social relationships with males and is a way to obtain social recognition from female peers and the public in general. She has become eroticized.

Soon she is having sex, and it is down hill from there.

Her young body is experiencing arousal and orgasm. Sexual activity becomes more frequent and academic success too often becomes a thing of the past; eroticization causes her to focus on her body and, as a result, her social life is centered around thoughts and plans that all come down to three things: her body, male attention, and sex. She and her sexual partners may or may not use condoms; she is playing sexual Russian roulette. Many of them will become pregnant and/or contract sexually transmitted diseases. Her peer group is popular with the boys, and as with the blind leading the blind, the immature and eroticized lead the immature and eroticized.

She is accustomed to and looks forward to comments about her body from boys and male adults. After a while, her relationship with her mother becomes strained because the daughter's behavior crosses parental authority boundaries. Mother accuses her of "acting too damn grown." Arguments and sometimes fights occur. The little girl is no longer "cute," and mother now wishes that daughter were not getting male attention.

If this mother-daughter relationship becomes too strained, the mother may attempt to have her daughter live with another relative, or she may simply put her out of the house or contact juvenile court to attempt to have her daughter locked up or placed on probation. Mother, even if she once thought certain behaviors exhibited by her daughter were cute, is now worried, angry, and scared. She senses that she has no control over her child. This girl's mother despises the boys that come to her home to visit her daughter; they remind her of the slick and deceiving men she has encountered. Mother is concerned that babies and/or sexually transmitted diseases will be a very likely outcome. Social service agencies and juvenile courts must eventually become involved in her family's life because the family is unable to handle it on their own.

Another common problem facing the eroticized Black female is the seductive advances of her mother's male companion (not her biological father). If this girl's mother has an unscrupulous boyfriend, he may take a sexual interest in her young daughter, especially if he knows that the daughter is already sexually active and notices how she seeks male attention. Though such a male would consider making sexual advances toward a non-eroticized girl, he will definitely make such advances toward the eroticized girl. This adult male may plan a way to win the young girl over, usually through monetary favors and flattery. He presents his seduction as joking and fun when in the presence of other family members. When he gauges that daughter is "ready" for him to approach her (meaning she will keep secrets), he then makes his sexual advance. Some of these men only stay with the mother as a way to

4

become sexual with her female child. Many mothers are unaware of the true meaning of some adult male kindness toward their physically developed female child and may inadvertently assist in delivering their daughter into the hands of an unscrupulous, predatory adult male.

When these girls reach age 18 to 21, they generally will have had dozens of sexual partners, even female sexual partners, and too many of them will have given birth to at least one child. Many who have not given birth have had abortions or miscarriages. The majority of these Black females will not have completed high school and will be enrolled in General Education Diploma (GED) classes. They will mostly reside in low-income projects and apartments and will begin to experience a great deal of bitterness with their lives.

This bitterness and frustration with their lives is evidenced by the following conditions: having babies with no financial or emotional support from the babies' daddies; working a low-paying job that does not allow them to get the material things they want or to move into better housing; inability to hire babysitters, thus hindering their ability to attend school, work, or social activities; meeting guys who only want to sex them (and possibly make more babies); and realizing that they have lost that sexy, male-attracting shape because of childbirth. It is not uncommon for some of these frustrated young Black mothers to shake and otherwise harm their babies. They are simply pissed off with their lives. And if they don't receive proper counseling, many will remain stuck in destructive thinking and destructive behaviors.

Let us now look at the eroticized Black boy. I believe that negative Rap songs and their accompanying videos often instill erotic sadism in the Black male child and adolescent. A sadist is someone who receives pleasure by inflicting pain, usually of a sexual nature, on others. This sadism and anger is manifested through expressed beliefs, attitudes, and behaviors. When a young Black boy takes pride in purchasing a shirt with the slogan "wife beater," it must not be taken as a passing fad. When a pre-teen or teenage African American male hears his favorite Rap idol, such as Ludacris, say "Get my d*** sucked…" and then hears Snoop Dogg rap about wearing Rolex watches, drinking expensive European alcoholic beverages, and referring to himself as a gangster, it effects the boy's belief and value system. The Black boy erroneously begins to believe that Rappers are in possession of the American dream because they wear expensive platinum jewelry, drive expensive cars, are strapped (carry a gun), f*** bad b*****s, and wear the latest brand-name clothes.

This misled Black male boy cannot afford the Rolex or cars or expensive jewelry; but he can get the girls. Girls become his vehicle for feeding his ego and imagination of himself in his Rap idol's image (this boy does not know that the Rapper has a White male gangster image in his own messed up mind). When he tries to "get with" Kiesha, he isn't concerned about anything except getting Kiesha to perform oral sex on him; to have sex with Kiesha in all the positions his Rap idols rap about; and then to brag to his misdirected, misled, misinformed, miseducated "niggahs" about how he "freaked that b****." Hurting and degrading the female becomes something to be proud of. The more females he can f***, deceive, and get money from, the merrier.

The eroticized Black male, in keeping with his Rap idols' instructions, must be "hard," meaning he must attempt to be void of all emotions except anger and must be willing to prove to others that he will sex a female or blow another Brother's brains out without a second thought. Caring for a "b****" is interpreted as being "soft" and must be avoided at all costs. Therefore, he prevents himself from truly loving a female. He is on the fast track to becoming an abusive adult male. A "hard" motherf***** can't love "them hos." Thugs don't love and cherish females. Gangsters don't love and cherish females (though our deluded young Brothers are anything but gangsters). As a result, the unfortunate females that become involved with these boys are initiated into a world of emotional and physical abuse. Some young girls are unaware that they are even being abused because they, too, are victims of this destructive eroticization and socialization.

This eroticized Black boy views the music videos on BET and becomes sexually aroused. As he focuses on confident Rappers "balling and shot-calling" with "fine a** hos" that are partially nude, their bodies oiled and gyrating in slow motion, he gets an erection and is likely to fantasize about having sex with the women on the videos or with a girl he has seen. When a 14-year-old Black boy rushes home to watch Beyonce's *Check On It* video, he has sex on his mind. At some point he will begin to seek out someone, preferably a girl who resembles the females in Rap videos. However, he is more likely to settle for whichever girl gives him the go-ahead. My experience as a counselor for juvenile sex offenders has revealed that some of these boys will even turn their sexual curiosity and desire toward a family member.

If this eroticized Black boy has a younger sister or a mentally retarded sister, it is a possibility that he will practice various sexual acts with her, performing oral sex, having sexual intercourse, taking nude pictures, etc. Years may pass before parents find out about this sexual molestation. A pre-adolescent or adolescent boy who becomes eroticized by Rap videos will seek a sexual outlet. He may begin to release his sexual tension by frequent masturbation, but eventually he will seek out the real thing. Ask a juvenile court judge or a family service supervisor in your city about the number of pre-adolescent and adolescent sex offenders that they know about, and I am certain you will be shocked.

Needless to say, the eroticized Black male-child quickly loses interest in school. He begins to earn straight A's in sexing the girls, wearing the latest name-brand clothing, cussing, fighting, smoking weed, and sometimes engaging in gang activities. If he graduates from high school, there is no movement from there. He will get a job and/or sell crack cocaine to his already dying Black neighborhood (the Black Village) and will probably have at least one child that he is not providing for. Though he is still listening to and admiring his Rap idols, he remains unable to see how these Rappers' songs, personalities, and videos have negatively impacted his life. By the time he reaches adulthood, he may be a drug addict; what can we expect him to be after years of smoking weed and drinking a "40"? Eventually, many of these misguided Brothers will end up in prisons, which are the new slave plantations.

The future of Blacks in America will become even bleaker as the conditions stated above increase. Brothers and Sisters, we have to not only debate this but we must *raise some hell about this!* The most difficult task will be challenging Rappers we like. I like Ludacris, but I don't like how he contributes to this madness. Do you understand how many Black girls and boys' life's ambition is to become a Rapper? And the majority of them are not thinking about a Will Smith type Rapper, No, they want to become the next Snoop Dogg or Lil Kim. The madness is contagious because Rappers have money and fame; the American Dream turned American Nightmare for Blacks.

MTV aired a cartoon version of Snoop Dogg accompanied by two-bikini-clad Black women in neck collars and chains. The show was called "Where My Dogs At?"

"With increasing regularity, child professors are accumulating evidence that suggests that children (pre-pubescent) are not only displaying sexual behavior but are doing so at younger and younger ages. Some of these behaviors are precocious in nature; sexual behaviors that are typically associated only with adolescence either occur with an unusually high frequency or are unnecessarily intrusive to others."

—Fred Kaser, Ed. D., from article, *Toward a Better Understanding of Children's Sexual Behavior*

2. The Hijacking of Children's Sexual Development

Most adults know that children have the capacity for sexual intimacy and that children do have sexual feelings. However, having the capacity for sexual activity is not the same as having mature, critical-thinking-based comprehension of sexuality. Children do not possess sexual knowledge, such as how the human body works, and they do not possess knowledge of the responsibilities and ramifications of engaging in sexual activities. After all, they are *children*. Simply because an 11-year-old Black girl or boy is able to engage in a sexual act, does not mean they are aware of the crucial ramifications of that act. Eroticized children and adolescents engage in sexual activity because they are sexually aroused, not because they are psychologically, emotionally, and financially *ready* to engage in sexual activity.

Sexually provocative Rap videos and songs hijack the normal sexual development of a child. This is not about sex being bad, but it is about sex being bad for children and adolescents. Sexual development in and of itself is natural and healthy, and it involves an intricate process, as stated here by Floyd M. Martinson:

> The sexual development of the child is complex, involving a number of factors. During its intrauterine period, the fetus exhibits sensory development that continues through the neonatal stage. The neonate is developing the capacity for intimacy through its interaction with its mother…. In the first year, the child exhibits increased interest in bodily exploration, as well as autoeroticism and the development of orgasmic abilities. In early childhood, there is increasing social interaction, especially with peers, that involves experimentation with sexual behaviors and intimacy. Gender roles and continued interactional sexual experimentation… develops through the preadolescent years, and during adolescence youth appear to learn sexual and intimate behaviors that enable them to function as adults in sexual encounters.

The Hijacking of Children's Sexual Development

Thus, children go through a normal development of their sexuality, and even when they reach adolescence (puberty), they are only able to *have sex* but are still *not ready to have sex.* It is important that we understand the difference between a physically developed girl or boy having sex and their readiness to have sex. Where is the critical thinking? Where is the understanding of consequences? Where is the understanding of male-female relationships? Where is the financial ability to provide for a child? These are absent. Though a bright adolescent may be able to talk a good talk about sex, he or she is definitely not able to and not ready to walk the walk of having children, providing for children, or paying for their own medical expenses.

It is, therefore, crucial that we understand the mental development of the child and adolescent in conjunction with their sexual development. The July 2005 "Harvard Mental Health Letter" states:

> Recent research has shown that human brain circuitry is not mature until the early 20s…. Among the last connections to be fully established are the links between the prefrontal cortex, seat of judgment and problem solving, and the emotional centers in the limbic system, especially the amygdala. These links are critical for emotional learning and high-level self-regulation.

Negative Rap songs, videos, and personalities (performers) whet the Black child's appetite for sexual activity at a time when the child or adolescent is not capable of utilizing good judgment and critical decision-making. This incomplete brain formation is the reason why a bright adolescent can answer questions about sex and drugs correctly but gives in to pressure and engages in sex or drugs. The "f******," "d*** s******," and "p***y licking" done by the "b*****s and hos" in the songs and sexually provocative videos only serve to instill intense curiosity and sexual arousal in the immature minds of Black child and adolescent viewers and listeners. The Black boy and girl begin to have sexual fantasies related to the Rap videos and songs. Our vulnerable children begin to wonder what it would feel like; what it would look like? What it would taste like? Who can I try it with? Where can I try it? Once a child begins to think like this, a parent is about to catch some hell. The parent often finds out after the fact, most often, way after the fact.

The "Harvard Mental Health Letter" goes on to state that: "Hormonal changes are at work, too. The adolescent brain pours out adrenal stress hormones, sex hormones, and growth hormone, which in turn influence brain development."

The combination of sexually stimulating videos and lyrics on immature, hormone-saturated adolescents is a recipe for disaster! While the child and adolescent is fantasizing about what it would feel like to engage

The Hijacking of Children's Sexual Development

in the various sexual acts mentioned in the songs and portrayed in the videos, they are likely to masturbate too much (more than twice per day). Understand that though masturbation is normal for developing children, the eroticized child will go to extremes and will simply masturbate with a frightening frequency. A non-eroticized 13-year-old child may masturbate sometimes and have sexual fantasies sometimes but not engage in sexual activities until age 19. However, an eroticized 13-year-old child will engage in sexual activity at age 13. As stated earlier, Rap videos and songs hijack healthy sexual development. The hijackers then take their victims on a premature sexual journey that too often leaves babies, diseases, and unrealized potential at journey's end.

Fred Kaeser, the Director of Health Services for Community School District Two in New York, writes:

> This increase in the sexual behavior of children should come as no surprise. We are after all, raising a generation of "super-sexualized" young people. Children around the country are exposed to an onslaught of sexual messages that come at them with the speed of lightening in all directions, and on an on-going basis. These sexual messages are frequently explicit, far too violent....

Though negative Rappers are not the only ones to blame, they play a major role in encouraging Black boys and girls to engage in sexual activities and violence and sometimes in violent sexual activities. And the fact that most of these negative Rappers are Black men and women makes the matter more sensitive because they know what Black neighborhoods are facing: teen pregnancy, AIDS, murder, drug addiction/dealing, etc.). One would expect them to eventually wake up and realize how they contribute to the destruction of their own people. Money and fame, however, can give rise to tunnel vision; and too many of our Black Rappers can only see the money.

Many sexually provocative rap videos are shown on BET right after school ends. Many Black boys and girls arrive home from school, turn on BET, and watch videos such as *Candy Shop,* by 50 Cent, and *Grillz*, by Nelly. The themes are generally developed around materialism and sex. After repeated exposure to many of the videos shown on BET, both girls and boys become curious about lesbian sex, threesomes, and orgies. Do not think for one minute that these videos are "only fun" and that no sexual arousal and sexual curiosity develop in our children. I mentioned the two videos above because they are videos by two of our most popular Rappers, and our children and grandchildren idolize these Rappers. You probably have no idea how many young girls have posters of 50 Cent on their bedroom wall.

16

The Hijacking of Children's Sexual Development

The hijacking of Black children's sexual development by Rap music videos and Rap songs leads to increased sexual activity among Black children. This then leads to babies having babies, and as you know, when young girls begin to birth children, there are all sorts of problems. Frances Cress Welsing, M.D., states

> Teenage motherhood presents many serious complications. Large numbers of these teenage mothers are poor and ignorant of medical needs. They do not receive adequate prenatal medical care or nutrition. Those girls in their early teens who become mothers are not physically fully developed and, therefore, they are less able to bear the physical strains of having a baby…have higher death rates, more anemia, more toxemia, more hemorrhage, and lower-weight babies….

How much more of this can the Black community afford before our ship is fully sunk, a ship that is already sinking. Since problems either become better or worse, it is imperative that Black men and women, regardless of whether you are someone's mother or father, take an action-oriented approach to stopping this destruction. Children and adolescents do not possess the necessary critical-thinking skills to see the cause-effect nature of not only Rap videos and

17

songs but also many other elements of life. As they cross the bridge from childhood to adulthood, we must prevent them from being sexually hijacked by people they love and look up to, people called Rappers.

The study, "Exposure to degrading Versus Non-degrading Music Lyrics and Sexual Behavior Among Youth," was conducted by the Rand Corporation, a nonprofit research organization. Research showed that songs with explicit references to sex acts that also depict men as "sex-driven studs" and women as sex objects are more likely to trigger early sexual behavior. The study recommends that parents set limits on what music their children can purchase and listen to.

3. Does BET Stand for "Black Eroticizing Television"?

Let's get straight to it.

Children and teens are generally very impressionable. Approval from their peer group is vital to their self-esteem. They are trying to fit in, to be perceived in a particular manner that is "aw-ight" (all right) with other kids. This is the reason many parents begin to have varying degrees of conflict as soon as their children enter middle school (6th, 7th, and 8th grades): puberty is kicking in. The adolescent wants adult privileges but not adult responsibilities. They often feel that parents don't understand or are too controlling. But in reality it is the developing adolescent who has not yet learned enough about life and truly does not understand. Now add vulgar, sexually provocative Rap lyrics and videos, specifically those seen on Black Entertainment Television (BET), to all of the above. The situation then becomes too much, too wrong, too soon, and it can't help but make one wonder if BET is really an acronym for Black Eroticizing Television.

Some people used to say, "The kids today got their thing the way we used to have our thing when we were young. It ain't that bad." They mean that those of us in our 40s, 50s, and even 60s went through the same kinds of things (behaviors) as today's teenagers are going through. The only truth about this statement is in terms of human development: We all went through various physical, mental, and emotional stages. And, of course, this will not change as long as humans are humans. However, much of the present musical and video material heard and seen in today's Rap is pathological.

This is the first time in history when recording artists/song writers call females b*****s and hos and glorify killing, drug use, and drug dealing. This is the first time in history when Black teens proudly sing about being members of gangs in which they kill other Blacks. When in the history of Black America did we hear such as the following:

> Niggas wanna run up in my p***y like a pap smear. I'mma tell you, just like I told you last year. Niggas ain't stickin' unless they lick the kitten, huh. Too many b*****s just be licking the d*ck and I'm a picky one. I like my d*cks rock hard.

The above lyrics are from Lil Kim's *Queen B**** Pt. II.* Is this healthy for Black children and adolescents? No, it is totally unhealthy. Would an 11, 12, 13, or 14-year-old Black girl become curious after hearing these lyrics? Would she wonder about oral sex and sexual intercourse? Would a 14-year-old Black boy wonder what it would be like to have a girl perform oral sex on him and to have sexual intercourse? The answer is yes to each question. The provocative dress

Does BET Stand for
"Black Eroticizing Television"?

of Lil Kim and some other female Rappers only serves to enforce the messages in their destructive songs and videos. Remember: children and teens are impressionable.

When Snoop Dogg sings, "I'm a bad boy, wit a lotta hos," many of his young Black male fans may seek to imitate this grown Black man who calls himself a dog and who has become famous for the way he calls females b*****s (beeeitch). After Black boys hear all or most of their favorite Rappers call females b*****s and hos, many of them will internalize these messages and begin to verbalize them and act them out. Many will come to believe that females are indeed b*****s and hos and will treat them as such. Understand that the mental process of *idolizing* a person is one of *worshipping* and, ultimately *becoming one with that person*. Most of the Rap videos shown on BET encourage these destructive dynamics.

It is important that you know about the BET program *Uncut*. Around 3:00 a.m., BET shows its most sexually provocative music videos. A black square hides some of the genitals. If you are thinking, "Well, most children should be asleep by 3:00 a.m., so this is no problem because only adults are watching these videos," you are partially correct—but mostly incorrect. Sixth, seventh, eighth, and ninth-graders *know* that these videos come on. And they figure out ways to see these videos. Don't be naïve; most children, when they really want to, are able to get around parental restrictions. Ask some youth that are under age 17 if they have ever seen BET's *Uncut*. The question must be asked: What is the reason why Black Entertainment Television shows programs such as *Uncut*? What kind of entertainment is BET trying to hook Black children and adolescents on?

Since children and adolescents, especially adolescents, function in groups, they often take on the proverbial act of the blind leading the blind. In other words, when a Black boy or girl is infected with negative Rap lyrics/video pathology, he or she is likely to infect peers. For example, if EJ begins to cuss around peers that admire him and then begins to wear his pants hanging off of his behind (sagging) and to refer to girls in school and in the neighborhood as hood rats, hos, and b*****s, he will more than likely be imitated by other members of his social group. It repeatedly comes to my mind that our Black children are being "sprayed" with a visual and verbal toxin (negative Rap videos and lyrics), and then they go into our "breeding" area (neighborhood) and spread the poison to others.

Ask some children and teenagers what they *feel* and what they *think* after viewing BET Rap videos. Don't put words into their mouths; allow them to talk candidly (you can work on helping them to correct their thinking only after learning how they think). When I ask this question during the various community-based groups I conduct, the boys almost always say such things as: "Man, them be some fine females on them

Does BET Stand for
"Black Eroticizing Television"?

videos"; "Can I talk real, Mr. Porter? Those hos fine as hell, Yo! Sh**, man, they be droppin' it like it's hot and a playa be wantin' it, Yo!"; "A niggah be dreamin' 'bout them b*****s, man."

These videos manipulate the sexual energy flowing through these adolescent boys and girls. The girls simply imitate the dress, attitude, and language (which includes lots of profanity) found in the videos and lyrics (don't deceive yourself into believing that the radio versions are what kids sing when parents are not around; *they know the real lyrics*). In short, these young Black male and female viewers are being set-up. Their hormones are literally leading them into experiences they are not able to handle. At the end of every BET Rap video there should be an HIV and teen pregnancy alert.

Many young boys idolize the Rapper named Lil Wayne. In one of Lil Wayne's videos, *Fireman*, he is obviously in a house of prostitution and is having sex with every female in the house. This video is blatant in its advocacy of sexual promiscuity. One message contained in *Fireman* is that females are on fire (wanting sex) and guys must use their penises to put out these sexual fires. With so many billboards across America's inner city areas warning African American males that HIV and AIDS are very real threats to all Black males, BET videos appear to deliberately seek to counter these warnings. Do BET's owners care?

My experience has been that the more Black children become immersed in Rap music and what is called hip-hop lifestyle, the worse their academics become. I believe that many Black youth have trouble shifting gears. In other words, they may speak and act in a certain way with peers, which is OK for that social group, but they are unable to change their style when facing a professional, a job interview, or an academic environment in which they must speak properly and cease clown-like behaviors. Too many Black youth become so comfortable wearing sagging pants that they truly have problems wearing belts around their waste, or wearing belts at all. It is bad enough that Black youth live within a racist social structure that seeks reasons to frustrate them; we cannot bear the further burden of pouring gasoline on the flames, as the saying goes.

Too many Black Rappers, such as Snoop Dogg, have difficulty making eye contact during interviews and have great difficulty with verbal expression. As is true in idol worship, too many Black males and females tend to look down or to the side instead of making eye contact. Too many Black teens and young adults tend to shuffle, droop their shoulders, and mumble when engaged in conversations with someone outside their peer group. BET only serves to encourage and to perpetuate this Zip Coon, Sambo behavior among African American children and teens through the Rap personalities and Rap videos they present.

Does BET Stand for
"Black Eroticizing Television"?

Acting silly in the peer group tends to be difficult to turn off for too many of our youth when they are on a job or in an environment where sport and play must be put on hold. Our misled, miseducated, misinformed Black teens have become human name-brand-wearing, billboard-vulgar, programmed-for-self-destruction Frankenstein creations. Their minds, to a large extent, are not their own. And negative Rap personalities, lyrics, and videos contribute to this sad condition. They are like Frankenstein creations because they have been "created" by Black male Rappers who are themselves imitating Al Pacino's character, Tony Montana, from the movie *Scarface*, and other real-life gangsters. Many Black teens are also Frankenstein creations because they are imitating Black male Rappers who call themselves by various Italian names and even name themselves after the Mafia.

I once asked a group of 19 Black male teens, while conducting a manhood development group for the Chatham County Department of Family and Children Services, "Who was Machiavelli?" I asked this question to make a point while discussing how the boys imitate a person they have no knowledge of, simply because a Rapper mentions or names himself after that person (in this case Tupac Shakur). None of the 19 Black male teenagers knew who Niccolo Machiavelli was. They gave the most ridiculous answers. Our kids' minds are not their own. Now, I would like to make some additional comments about Black Entertainment Television (BET).

Instead of the BET acronym meaning Black Entertainment Television, it should mean Black Eroticizing Television. BET contributes to the eroticizing of Black children. BET shows videos that resemble what the adult film industry calls soft porn. BET is the Rapper's visual vehicle for reaching their Black child and adolescent audience. We must wonder if the top executives of BET understand the murder rates, incarceration rates, sexual offense rates, HIV infection rates, teen pregnancy rates, and unemployment rates of their Black child and adolescent viewers? If they do understand, we should expect them to show programs designed to decrease and to prevent the destruction of Black children, not just to profit from manipulating them.

Hundreds of thousands, if not millions, of Black children nationwide cannot wait to get home from school to watch BET Rap videos. Many of these children are able to watch BET's late night Rap videos, which are off the chain in terms of being sexually provocative. It is no secret that many parents work at night and are unable to prevent their children from watching these sexually charged Rap videos. Two of my clients come to mind. One was a male teenage client who was caught by his mother masturbating in the den to a video on BET. He later confessed to frequently

Does BET Stand for
"Black Eroticizing Television"?

masturbating to Rap videos shown on BET. A second adolescent male client, 15 years old, frequently masturbated to pornographic magazines, which he also took to school. After the magazines were taken from him, it was later discovered (and he confessed to this) that he began to masturbate while watching *Rap City* on BET. He needed this visual stimulation to fuel his sexual fantasies, and *Rap City* provided this fuel.

Do the executives at BET know about the HIV and AIDS rates among Black youth? The February 10, 2006, issue of the "MMWR Weekly," published by the Center for Disease Control, cited research in 33 states done from 2001 to 2004, which states that of the 531 female children under age 13 with HIV/AIDS, 368 were Black. Of the 129 females ages 13 to 14 with HIV/AIDS, 106 were Black. Of 6,592 females ages 15 to 24 with HIV/AIDS, 4,615 were Black. What in hell are BET executives thinking? Don't they know that the videos shown on BET contribute to this destruction of Black youth? Or do they intend to just continue to eroticize Black youth?

I understand that many Blacks love and appreciate BET and do not like such criticism of their programming, but it is vital to the well-being of Black children that we take the approach that no one is beyond reproach when it comes to saving Black children. To put it very clearly: Lots and lots of children become sexually excited from watching Rap videos on BET and begin to fantasize (some of these children act out their sexual fantasies) about all types of sexual acts. Entertaining Black children should not be synonymous with destroying Black children.

"Children of the Gone. Lost and forgotten.
Minds rotten. The R Kay shot 'em.
Channel zero on the TV got em."
—Public Enemy, from their song, *Unstoppable*

4. Tweening

Corporate America pimps children. I could say they "manipulate" children, but the word manipulate is not strong enough to explain what corporate America really does: Pimp children. The Black child is virtually attacked from land, air, and sea. The Black child is "tweened." What is tweening and how does it contribute to the eroticizing and destruction of Black children?

Juliet Schor, author of *Born to Buy: The Commercialized Child and the New Consumer Culture* (2004), explains that many American corporations that once targeted products such as make-up, jeans, perfume, and other items to older adolescents, now target 8 to 12-year-olds. This is called "tweening." The purpose of tweening is to get much younger kids to crave items and then literally nag parents into purchasing these items. Juliet Schor states:

> The average American child is exposed to 40,000 advertising messages each year, according to recent estimates, and corporations are currently spending $15 billion annually

advertising and marketing to kids up to age
12...to promote entertainment, fashion and
apparel, electronics and furniture, and health
and beauty aids." (*Washington Post*, 2004)

The advertisers are winning the war for the
minds of children. It is very difficult to avoid
advertising; therefore, it becomes very difficult to avoid
its influence and effect. The $15 billion dollars being
spent by corporations is effectively turning Black
children into money-spending addicts. When you hear
an adult say that a child is "acting grown," what is
often taking place is the inappropriate expression of
fashion/dress and/or attitude by the child. "Grown" is
a condition of adulthood; it is not a time of "play-play."
When children are tricked by corporate advertisers into
"acting grown," they are also prone to act grown
sexually. It does not stop with fashion. Sometimes,
various fashions (i.e., low-cut jeans on females that
allow thong straps to be viewed) encourage sexual
behaviors.

Tweening is a crucial part of a child-focused
marketing strategy called age compression. Juliet Schor
states:

Age compression includes offering teen
products and genres, pitching gratuitous
violence to the twelve-and-under crowd,
cultivating brand preference for items that were

previously unbranded among younger kids, and developing creative alcohol and tobacco advertising that is not officially targeted to them but is widely seen and greatly loved by children.

The sponsors of shows viewed by older adults, young adults, and teens *know* and *desire* to have the children and relatives of these adults and teens present when various shows are on television. These corporations want seven-year-old boys to ask parents to purchase $100 pairs of Jordan's. These wickedly wise corporations know that young children are not into brands, but they are determined to mentally program these children into becoming consumer zombies by any means necessary. Rap videos and songs often include Rappers bragging about drinking various liquors, beer, and wine and smoking marijuana or cigarettes such as Black and Mild and Swisher Sweets. This entices children who previously had no interest in or knowledge of various alcohol and tobacco products to become curious about these products.

Remember: Rap has become a tool used by corporations to help them to pimp Black children. The fashion industry, as well as the alcohol and tobacco industries, relies on Rappers to help them trap and exploit Black children. Are Rappers aware of this dynamic? I believe that most of them are not aware. Some are aware but simply don't give a damn as long as they "get paid." Others, such as Kanye West, Public Enemy, and Will Smith, do care about Black people.

Juliet Schor states:

> By the time many children reach early elementary school, they have already been incorporated into the universe of junk entertainment, listening to music, and watching movies and television that offer them unprecedented levels of violence along with the presentation of young people as sexual objects.

Our children are being killed before having a chance to grow. They are the victims of menticide, a term used by Bobby E. Wright, which means: "The deliberate and systematic destruction of a person or group's mind." (1984) Black children are being instilled by television, movies, and their favorite Rappers with a desire to kill. Many Rappers rap about killing other Black people with Glocks and AK 47's and pistol whipping others. Third- and fourth-graders are using the words "fine" and "sexy" to describe Beyonce, Bow Wow, Lil John, 50 Cent, Lil Kim, and many other Rappers. This may sound cute to some people, but it is anything but cute. These idols have been presented to their young fans as sexual objects, and since idolizing someone ultimately means attempting to become like him or her, millions of Black six-, seven-, and eight-year-olds will utilize fashion, language (vulgar), and attitude in their efforts to become sexy.

Public schools report third- and fourth-grade girls perform oral sex on boys in school restrooms. Principals contact parents about sending elementary children to school wearing short, tight jean skirts and sagging pants. Schools complain that too many children are rude and disrespectful in their speech and demeanor. Some teachers are well meaning and have the best interest of Black children at heart. But let's not say the problem is totally the parents' fault. Sure, some parents need help, but this kind of behavior exhibited by children is widespread and is not brought about by a lack of parental involvement in the child's life. The $15 billion that corporations spend to exploit and pimp children makes certain that parents are quickly neutralized and rendered almost defenseless in preventing the mental kidnapping of their children.

Does eroticizing and exploitation of our children make them anxious, angry, and depressed? Yes, it does. Remember: Children may take on certain attitudes, beliefs, and behaviors, but they are not able to *conceptualize* and to *comprehend* the *reason* why they act as they do. This is frustrating, scary, and confusing to children. Most of them are not able to stop because they don't even know *how* it happened. Imagine how you would feel if you had no idea why you were doing things; wouldn't you feel anxious and scared? Juliet Schor writes:

While the figures tell me children's well-being was affected by consumer involvement, they do not explain how. One possibility is that people who are envious of others and worried about possessions and money are more likely to be depressed and anxious. Desiring less—rather than getting more—seems to be the key to contentment and well-being. Perhaps, as they focus on the consumer culture, kids spend less time in the reading and play that keeps them happy and healthy. Difficult as it is to explain, the connection is clear: The more enmeshed children are in the culture of getting and spending, the more they suffer for it.

The age compression and tweening of children goes against nature. Whenever anyone goes against nature, something abnormal happens; something bad happens; something goes wrong. The $15 billion spent by corporations to exploit children is basically used to defy the nature of human development. The money is used to create little child Frankensteins, children whose minds are not their own. When Rappers brag about expensive cars, expensive name-brand clothes, expensive jewelry, and expensive sneakers, they are directly contributing to the destruction of their own people by whetting the appetites of poor Black kids for items they cannot afford. Kanye West did a video on the exploitation of children in Africa by the diamond-mining corporations that should be viewed and studied by all Rappers.

Little Black girls and boys will reject reading and healthy play when they are lured into the eroticizing process. Little Black girls would not have the pressure of figuring out how to reveal breasts, behinds, and legs to equally confused little Black boys (and grown men) if corporations and the Rappers pimping for these corporations would leave them alone. But the money earned from disrupting childhood is too good to resist. After all, why should corporate America give a damn about Black children? Juliet Schor Writes:

> How have things gotten so far out of hand? For the last decade, the kids junk culture has been relentlessly pushed by a small number of mega-corporations—Viacom, Disney, McDonald's, Burger King, Philip Morris, Coca-Cola, Pepsi, Sony Pictures, and others. Through their advertising agencies, these companies have developed sophisticated and effective methods of reaching children that go far beyond the television ads of yesteryear.

She goes on to reveal a very calculated marketing strategy:

That kind of intensive research went into companies figuring out they could turn shampoo bottles into licensed character toys, plastic first-aid bandages into "tattoos," and ketchup into a gross green goop that kids will demand. Marketers have also perfected stealth marketing efforts, such as "peer-to-peer" campaigns that enlist kids to market to their friends and schoolmates, a process that has been gaining popularity recently.

This is frighteningly deadly in its impact on the Black community in America. We cannot withstand this type of sophisticated assault on our children. Many of us have no clue as to what is happening and how corporations do it. Economically prostituted Black children are used to influence other Black children; the blind leading the blind into the monster's lair. And many Black Rappers are lending a helping hand, assisting their Brothers and Sisters in going to hell in a hand basket. When our most valued resource, Black children, is exploited in a manner that teaches them how to deliver other Black children into the hands of people who have never cared about Blacks, we must take no-nonsense measures to put an end to this. Death is being delivered to Black children under the guise of entertainment and fun and a carefree lifestyle. Death with a smiley face, concealing a malicious cancer, hell bent on destroying the minds, bodies, and souls of Black children.

5. Sexualized America

The United States of America's corporations specialize in manipulating the sexual nature of humans for profit. It's true: sex sells. Magazines at grocery stores and Wal-Mart checkout counters carry cover stories about the sexiest men and women alive. Descriptions of entertainers, athletes, and presidential candidates often include the word "sexy." Automobiles are described as sexy. Behind the counters of convenience stores and gas stations are adult sex magazines (pornography). And, of course, fashions must be sexy if they are to be purchased. America is a sexualized nation, and our children and teens are its perennial victims. A sexualized America produces sexualized children, and sexualized children have problems.

Before children even develop the most remote misconception of sex, they are given Barbie Dolls (Barbie's shape is that of an adult female, and her blond-haired, blue-eyed image is unhealthy for Black girls); the Bratz (which wear sexually provocative clothing, push the blond, blue-eyed, bi-racial image, are targeted to elementary-age girls, and like Barbie are unhealthy for Black girls), and other sexualized toys to play with. Through playing with these dolls, children, especially Black girls, internalize the physiques, hair texture/color, skin color, and eye color of the dolls. Is there any wonder that many Black girls and Black female entertainers have blond hair and wear gray, blue, and hazel contact lenses?

The sexualized child will engage in sex at a young age. First, there is exposure through television, "sexy" toys, sitcoms, song lyrics, and music videos. Second, there is curiosity. Third, there is sexual fantasy (often coupled with too frequent masturbation). Fourth, there is finding someone to sexually experiment with. Fifth, there is engagement in sexual acts (if the child is also viewing BET videos, sexual acts will include threesomes and bisexuality).

The scary part of this is that parents often cannot see it happening. This process rises like the tide; it is up to your ankles and before you know it, above your knees. Few parents ever stop to think about the toy female with the hourglass figure and the tight, sexually provocative clothing. Many parents think their children are too young or too innocent to view these toys as anything other than toys, but the marketers know, and the results are dangerous.

According to Fred Kaeser,

> We know that exposure to sexualized messages, particularly those that are incomprehensible, have several effects on children. They can raise many questions and cause considerable confusion. Parents today are in an unenviable position of having to deal with certain sexual issues at earlier ages with children than parents

just ten years ago. Excessive exposure to sexual messages can cause some children's typical curiosity about sex to become increasingly distorted, particularly when parents and adults fail to intervene. All children are curious about things that are sexual. With continual exposure, however, we know that there are some children who run the risk of becoming too preoccupied with sexual matters. Some children will act out the sexual messages they are exposed to. Some children will utilize their sexualized behavior to hurt other children.

America is producing out-of-control children. When a child's sexual curiosity gradually becomes an obsession, many bad things will occur. Academic success takes a back seat to sex. Parental advice takes a back seat to sex. Repeated exposure to sexual messages and to sexual images causes the child to develop a sexual fixation. Sexual arousal engulfs the child. Some of these children will engage in sexual activity with unscrupulous adults, with both older and younger children (sexual offenses occur at this point), and with animals (usually family pets). They will text message and e-mail messages of a highly sexual nature to both those they know and to total strangers. These children will seek sexual outlets and will find them. Parents are often the last to know. Remember: this destructive sexualization process rises like the tide.

A very sick American society sends children the very strong message that their life is about how their body looks and how they use it and allow others to use it. The children are conditioned to prostitute themselves at the altars of television, music videos, video games, shopping malls, and the streets. Children, hypnotized by the sexual lure of American media and the fashion industry, charge full steam ahead into that which they do not understand and are not ready to deal with.

Sexualized America produces sex offenders. I predict that by 2010 the number of young (12 years of age and older) sex offenders will substantially increase in the United States. Follow this process: An 11-year-old boy or girl gets sexually aroused by certain Rap videos or television shows. She/he begins to masturbate two to three times per day; fantasies always accompany masturbation (sexual thoughts of someone known or not known by the child). The 11-year-old child is alone at home playing with a 7-year-old cousin, and no adults are in the room. The 11-year-old asks or entices or forces the younger cousin to engage in oral sex or anal sex with him/her. This happens five times before someone catches them or when the 7-year-old begins to exhibit strange behaviors of a sexual nature toward other children or adults, and it is brought to the parents' attention and the 7-year-old is questioned.

Sexualized America encourages events such as Ladies' Night; Wet Tee Shirt Night; Bikini Night; and many other socially acceptable occasions that promote the image of females as entertainment. It is no wonder that pornography flourishes in American society. Presented as fun, these and other such activities (e.g., strip clubs) fuel lust and gives rise to a self-perpetuating climate of sexual abandon. What is abandoned? Care, self-discipline, commitment, self-respect, respect for others (especially for females), and concern about consequences. Concrete examples are date rapes, fraternity "gang bangs" of females on university campuses, and filming sexual activity with a female without her knowledge or consent, then showing it to one's buddies as they down a few kegs.

The people with the authority to determine what is produced and what is shown on television, in magazines, and on the Internet have the power to push their sexual preferences onto others. They are mostly White male executives. If they are homosexual, they can give a green light to sitcoms that mix homosexual lifestyles with humor. It is these White men who will allow characters on the television show *Girlfriends* to use the words "bitches" and "kiss my a**." This show is watched by lots of young, Black females and males. Children and teens, especially children, often believe that if it is said or done on television, then it is OK to say and do it in public. On the television show *Everybody Loves Raymond*, you are not likely to hear the words "b****" and "kiss my a**."

In her book *Pornified: How Pornography Is Transforming Our Lives, Our Relationships, and Our Families*, Pamela Paul talks about a 27-year-old music executive, whom she calls Ethan, and his love of pornography. A music executive has the power to have recording artists do the things the music executive likes. Ethan likes pornography that features 18- to 20-year-old blond females. He especially likes lesbian sex, oral sex, and "cum shots." Think about the Rap lyrics and Rap videos shown on television, especially Black Entertainment Television. Take a serious look at 50 Cent's *Candy Shop* video, among many others by different so-called artists. Maybe there are many Ethans in the music industry.

Snoop Dogg has produced several XXX-rated videos that are only sold in adult video stores. Now think about it: The most popular Rapper is producing pornographic videos that depict group sex, threesomes, lesbian sex, and damn near anything else you can imagine. Do not think for one second that our children are not aware that Snoop Dogg makes pornographic videos. They know, and they would like to see them. I don't know if this Brother is aware that he is probably encouraging hundreds of thousands of Black kids to seek out pornography. If Snoop Dogg doesn't know this, I hope he knows about the HIV, pregnancy, and murder rates among Black teens across America. And I hope Snoop Dogg and other prominent Rappers are able to make the connection between their lyrics and behaviors and how their Black male and female fans may imitate them.

Pamela Paul states:

> Pornography is frequently the first place boys learn about sex and gain an understanding of their own sexuality, whims, preferences, and predilections—their desires filtered and informed by whatever the pornography they watch has to offer. As adolescents, many boys learn through pornography to direct their sexual feelings toward the opposite sex, to explain the source of the desires and the means to satisfy them—lessons traditionally supplemented by sex education, parental guidance, peer conversation, and real-life experience. Whether mediated by outside sources or not, the pornography lesson is nothing if not straightforward; most is geared toward the adolescent mind: simple, primal, hormone-driven, results-oriented, a winnable game.

Is America producing generations of sexually fixated children? Are Black Rappers, such as Snoop Dogg, unknowingly participating in the production of sexually confused, sexually misguided Black girls and boys, some of whom will undoubtedly become sexual offenders and victims of sexual abuse? The answer is "yes." This dysfunctional train has already left the station and is derailing as you read these words.

Male-female relationships in sexualized America have become intensely superficial. When the sexual nature of humans is corrupted, relationships become corrupted. Listen to Pamela Paul:

> Pornography has a corrosive effect on men's relationships with women and a negative impact on male sexual performance and satisfaction. It plays a rising role in intimacy disorders. More than ever, it aids and abets sexually compulsive behavior in ways that can become seriously disruptive and psychologically damaging.

With all the problems plaguing the Black community, we can ill afford an increase in juvenile sex offenders, teen mothers, HIV rates, and single motherhood. The soft porn nature of many Rap videos is a gateway to more graphic pornography and hence is destructive to the development of healthy male-female relationships.

The African Village cannot go down, *must* not go down with a morally sick, consumer-saturated, sex-crazed America. I remember Harry Belafonte explaining that his mentor, Dr. Martin Luther King, Jr., stated that Blacks are integrating into a house that is morally on fire; meaning that White America's morals were harmful to Blacks. Dr. King would be utterly disappointed today, as would Malcolm X, who warned us that we were making a grave mistake. Pamela Paul continues:

Sexualized America

A 2004 poll of 15,246 men and women conducted by MSNBC.com and *Elle* magazine documented that three-fourths of the men said they had viewed or downloaded erotic films and videos from the Internet. (Forty-one percent of the women did as well.) One in five men had watched or sexually interacted with someone on a live webcam. Three in ten admitted they go online with the intention of "cheating on their girlfriends or wives," be it via pornography, online dating, or sex chat rooms.

This toxic soup—consisting of daytime soap operas that are becoming more and more sexually provocative; sitcoms that humorously interject gay lifestyles into their themes; sitcoms that contain profanity; Rap videos that sexually arouse Black boys and girls; popular shows, such as *The Sopranos,* that mix sex and violence; and magazines that feature Black women wearing blond hair, colored contact lenses, and very little clothing—is filling the minds of hundreds of thousands of pre-adolescent and adolescent males and females.

Again, death disguised with a smiley face is being delivered to us via print and electronic media; the fashion industry; toy manufacturers; and the popular entertainers that millions of children and teens look up to. Young Black girls learn to accentuate behinds and breasts before they learn algebra. Young Black boys learn about bitches, hos, and Glocks before learning to write an essay. Too many of our children have as their life's goal to become sexy and popular. And some will attempt to become sexy and popular by any, and I mean *any,* means necessary!

6. When Pathology Becomes a Norm: Hip-Hopping into Madness

Generally, when people use the words "normal" and "abnormal," their reference points are behaviors shown (normal) or not shown (abnormal) by *most* people in that society. Here is an example: It is normal that people in American society put on a belt with pants or jeans and position the belt around the waist. It was once considered strange or weird or "abnormal" for someone to deliberately put on a pair of pants that dropped to their groin area due to not wearing a belt. However, since popular culture idols (athletes, Rappers, movie stars) began to wear their pants and jeans in sizes so large that the jeans hung below their waste at groin level, it has become "normal." Here's my point: Even though people may say that something is perverted or abnormal, they tend to accept the perversion or abnormality when the media (popular culture) and popular entertainers and athletes embrace the perverted or abnormal behaviors. When people we look up to do something, then it must be OK. Genuine pathology, which is an illness, is unfortunately accepted as a norm in America. In this chapter, we will examine this and will also look at pathological language.

As it relates to hip-hop, it is a sad commentary on the state of Black America that Rappers glorify violence (Black-on-Black murder), use the words b****, ho, and motherf***** in every song, and become award-winning "artists" (and they have the audacity to thank God for this "achievement" during award shows). If Black communities across America were not plagued with murder (mostly Black males), teen pregnancy, family destruction, AIDS, and high incarceration rates, then maybe, and only *maybe,* this would not be such a serious moral dilemma.

However, moral dilemmas often give rise to physically destructive problems; often one cannot exist without the other. Black reality is plagued with all the problems stated above. Black children receive a powerful message that since this behavior is rewarded (Rappers obtain wealth and fame), it is OK to engage in these behaviors. Instead of being seen as sick and destructive to the well-being of the Black community, it is viewed as cool and being "down." This is hip-hop turned madness.

When Eminem sings, "Oh, now he's raping his own mother, abusing a whore, snorting coke, and we gave him the Rolling Stone cover? You goddamn right B****, and now it's too late. I'm triple platinum and tragedies happen in two states " (Eminem from his song *Kill You*), we should criticize this as being "sick" in its effect on Black children and teens Or when Ludacris sings, "Hit the stage and knock the curtains down. I f*** the crowd up—that's what I do. Young and successful—a sex symbol. The b*****s want me to f*** 'em—true, true. Hold up, wait up, shorty Oh aww wazzzup? Get my d*ck sucked, what are you doin'?"

When Pathology Becomes a Norm:
Hip-Hopping into Madness

(Ludacris from his song *Move B*****), or when Da Brat sings, "They know just what I want and need. Keep a big bank roll and a bag of weed," we should sharply and frequently criticize these artists for contributing to the destruction of Black lives.

At the conclusion of his book *The Hip-Hop Generation*, Bakari Kitwana writes,

> A working unified front would greatly en-
> hance rap's potential to contribute to needed
> sociopolitical transformations. The real ques-
> tion is this: why should hip-hop generationers
> continue to participate in and support a mul-
> tibillion dollar industry if it fails to in any way
> address the critical problems facing our genera-
> tion? What good is rap music if it does nothing
> more than give young Blacks the opportunity
> to "dance to our own degradation" as ...Maulana
> Karenga has noted and if it enriches only a few
> at the expense of the many?

Ponder these questions: Do Rappers (other than positive Rappers such as Public Enemy and KRS-One) read? If so, what are they reading? Of course, I don't know if Snoop Dogg, Scarface, Lil Wayne, or 50 Cent read books or not, but I don't think they read such authors as Maulana Karenga, Na'im Akbar, Jawanza Kunjufu, Akil, Frances Cress-Welsing, or Amos N. Wilson. They probably haven't even read *The*

Hip-Hop Generation, by Kitwana. If they have read or are reading any of these authors or other authors of such tremendous insight and quality, it is not showing in their lyrics or in their videos. So, what kinds of information are Rappers putting into children's minds? My guess is: violent movies; visual images of White gangsters—real and imagined (i.e., Al Capone, Tony Montana); visual images of Rolls Royce, Hummers, and Jaguars; visual images of expensive name-brand clothes; and little else.

Most Rappers do absolutely nothing to better Black folk when they disseminate information and advice that is specifically geared to thwart the resurrection of the Black nation. They only make Willie Lynch proud through their role of assisting in the negative programming of young Black girls and boys. Instead of helping Black girls and Black boys to become competent, responsible Black adults, they are helping them to become thugs, gangsters, b*****s, and hos.

We are rewarding money-crazed, mentally blind-deaf-and-dumb Black men, women, and adolescents for destroying their own people, in their roles as negative Rappers. It is our Black boys who are imitating fictional characters from movies such as *Scarface.* It is our Black boys and girls who are calling themselves gangsters and thugs and are all too often acting out their pathological beliefs. It is our Black boys who are bragging about busting a cap in a nigga's a** with their Glocks or AKs. Too many of our Black

When Pathology Becomes a Norm:
Hip-Hopping into Madness

girls are proudly calling themselves b*****s and hos and allowing themselves to be treated as such by miseducated Black males. We are on a downward spiral into death and destruction, and we are Rapping and laughing and clowning as we go. This, Brothers and Sisters, is pathology.

When the White power structure, which owns, operates, and controls America's airwaves, views the Black community in America accepting sexually degrading and violent entertainment directed at Black youth, it knows that it, the power structure, will never have to worry about Black America producing another Malcolm X or Elijah Muhammad or Marcus Garvey or Martin Luther King. They know there will be no more women such as Fannie Lou Hammer, Mary McCloud Bethune, Betty Shabazz, Rosa Parks, or Coretta Scott King; only booty shakers and thugs will take center stage in Black America. When vulgar, violence-glamorizing Black adolescent and adult entertainers are idolized and given rewards, those who oppress us know that there is no longer anything whatsoever to fear from African Americans. We are checkmated.

America's White power structure is well aware that Blacks fell into a coma during the 1970s. When we awoke in the 1980s, we opened our eyes to the hell of closed Black-owned businesses, drug-infested communities, gang violence, accelerated family deterioration, high rates of teen pregnancy, AIDS, and high incarceration rates on America's new slave plantations called prisons.

We have been forming committees, meeting with American presidents, voting, rebuilding the NAACP, and doing almost any other thing you can think of in our efforts to get back on track. However, there is much against us. We find delight in being part of mainstream American entertainment; it makes us feel good, as if we have arrived or will soon be arriving. Arriving where? To that magical place where Black folk are just other Americans, not Black, but just other Americans, just like White folk.

Though we did not like Halle Berry earning an Oscar for *Monster's Ball*, we celebrated. Though we would have preferred our much loved Brother, Denzel Washington, to have received the Oscar for *Hurricaine* or *Malcolm X* instead of for *Training Day*, we celebrated. And then we have Snoop Dogg, 50 Cent, Lil Kim, and other Rappers that give totally unhealthy images and messages to Black kids, and still we celebrate because we are so happy to "be there." Malcolm X explained that of all the horrors Whites have inflicted upon Blacks, the worst is teaching Blacks to hate themselves. Think about it.

Would the children of a people who love themselves take pride in bragging about how they kill each other, sexually degrade their females, use drugs, sell drugs, and then dress in a deplorable manner? No.

When Pathology Becomes a Norm:
Hip-Hopping into Madness

If our children loved themselves, and if Black adults loved themselves, we would not allow our children to engage in such self-hating acts, even if they were well-paid to do so. If Black youth and Rappers loved themselves, they would be embarrassed to engage in this damaging process. If Black youth and Black entertainers loved themselves, they would not dye their hair blond or add blond weave to their hair or change their eye color. This is self-hatred. The White owners of media have no problem paying self-hating Blacks lots of money, making them millionaires, in order to control the masses of Black people. Money, for the White power structure, is truly no object.

Understand that simply because someone is rich and famous does not mean that they cannot suffer from self-hatred. The act of normalizing that which is pathological leads us to believe that vulgar, violence-advocating Rappers and blond-haired Blacks with light-colored contact lenses are worthy of being emulated and imitated. It is not too far-fetched to state that we *almost* have a generation of Black boys that want to become Rappers. The number of Black girls desiring to become Rappers is increasing, too. This is not good. How many Snoop Doggs and 50 Cents can Blacks handle? On the road to becoming a famous, rich Rapper, how many Blacks will our boys kill (a Rapper has got to have a bad reputation)? How much dope will they have to smoke? How many times will they have to be shot or arrested in order to show that they are "down"?

A sick mind, just as a healthy mind, thinks in terms of words and their meanings. There is healthy verbal-thought-related language and there is unhealthy verbal-thought-related language. The language contained in negative Rap songs is unhealthy and facilitates the development of an unhealthy mind and, consequently, unhealthy behaviors. American society, including we African Americans, has condoned and, subsequently, normalized pathology-based language in hip-hop as cool and fine for general usage. However, "b****," "nigger," "ho," "dog," "hood rat," "thug," "gangster," and some other terms commonly used by Black Rappers and their audience (Black children and teens) are dangerous. And here are the reasons.

Language is internalized into one's belief system. After repeated usage through general conversation/social interaction and through enter-tainment, the language evokes behaviors. In other words, many Black boys and girls actually view themselves as niggers, hos, b*****s, gangsters, thugs, and hood rats—and they act accordingly. The result is continued and worsened problems in Black commu-nities. Too many Black boys develop a Glock-penis-name-brand-bad-attitude way of living and of interacting with others. It is so cool on Rap videos but so deadly on the 11 o'clock news. Problems at school

When Pathology Becomes a Norm: Hip-Hopping into Madness

become frequent. Physical aggression becomes frequent. Disrespect of self and of others becomes the norm.

The normalizing of pathology is literally destroying Black folk. Too many of us are afraid to complain and to just straight-out verbally attack this madness because we see so many prominent Blacks and Whites supporting the madness. Regardless, we should *verbally attack* the madness. This situation is too crucial for sugar coating: this problem must be *attacked!* If Jewish American children were being destroyed, would Jewish Americans attack the problem? If Japanese American children were being destroyed, would Japanese Americans attack the problem? Would these and other groups simply sit back and accept the destruction of their children? No, they would not.

The African American community must begin to assertively and consistently criticize its Rappers, actors, and athletes that either knowingly or unknowingly (don't assume that simply because someone is rich and famous they have *consciousness*) participate in normalizing pathological behaviors and language that only serve to facilitate Black incarceration, Black poverty, Black sexual offenses, Black HIV rates, Black murder, and Black family deterioration. Each Black person has a responsibility to help other Black people. If we deceive ourselves into believing otherwise, we will be checkmated by a social-economic-military system that could care less about Black life. In other words, if we don't believe that we are responsible for each other, then we are suicidal, and a suicidal mind is a sick mind.

Suicidal people kill themselves because they are in emotional and psychological pain and are seeking an outlet, an escape. The normalizing of pathological behaviors and pathological ideas/beliefs eventually destroys those who practice those beliefs and behaviors because they eventually give rise to emotional and psychological pain. Sickness can only be ignored for a while, and even though one may ignore sickness, sickness takes its toll on the sick person.

When pathology becomes the norm in a society, that which is normal becomes "old fashioned," "country," "square," "nerdy," "plain," "simple," and "out-dated." Healthy, life-enhancing values become something people used to believe, but do not anymore. This is dangerous for Black kids, not only because children and adolescents want to fit in—and too many adolescents would do anything to fit in—but also because Blacks are historically and currently stereotyped as immoral, lustful, and violent by White-dominated society. And White society would not hesitate to add yet another layer to the stereotypes of Blacks. Let us be aware of this. Understanding all of the above is absolutely necessary for saving ourselves.

"To all my motherf*****' gettin' money hos
used to clothes"
—Lil Kim from her song *Suck My D*ck*

"You want this money then you gotta be a Badd b****
Shake that a** for a tip if you a Badd b****"
—Ying Yang Twin's from their song *Badd*

"Lil man with the big checks
Lil man that's got big girls
Wanting to teach me about sex"
—Lil Bow Wow from his song *The Dog in Me*

7. Does Your Daughter Want To Be a "Video Ho"?

Question: Do Black girls admire the female models seen in Rap videos? Answer: Yes, Black girls do admire the female models they see in Rap videos. What do Black girls admire about these video models, who are commonly referred to as "video hos" in the Rap industry? They admire their light skin complexions, their long flowing hair, their blond hair (Blacks with blond hair), their small waists and well-formed behinds, the attention popular Rappers give them, and the way boys in school and in the neighborhood talk about how much they desire these video models.

57

Since Black girls' favorite Rappers use Black females such as those described above, many Black girls develop the belief that if they can only look like the video models, they too would gain the attention of popular guys at school, in shopping malls, and in their neighborhoods. This belief is further strengthened when Black girls view popular entertainers such as Beyonce, Lil Kim, Mary J. Blige, and others who wear blond hair and/or hazel-colored contact lenses. In the minds of too many Black girls, they must, literally, do a total makeover, in which they change their physical selves into the desired image of the loved, cherished, and desired "other."

Rappers are Black men/adolescents who tend to choose females for their videos that are as close to White as possible. If she is Black, she has to be "pretty" and Black, which means that she must have keen facial features and long, flowing hair; she must look like a White girl dipped in light chocolate. To be a video model she must also, of course, wear her clothes tight or revealing or both. She must be sexy and must move as provocatively as allowed by law. Young Black girls and teens, sometimes beginning in fourth or fifth grade, ask their parents to perm their hair, to purchase weave so they can have "long" hair, to dye their hair blond, and to purchase blue or gray or hazel-colored contact lenses. They have now begun to imitate and to emulate Rap video models.

Does Your Daughter Want To Be a
"Video Ho"?

Young Black girls and teens then start to dress as "sexy" as allowed by parents and school dress codes. Jeans are ultra-tight. Navels and breasts are revealed at every opportunity. Tattoos are strategically placed on lower backs, cleavage (some of them don't even have breasts yet), necks, navels, and buttocks. With all of this come a certain attitude and a certain way of thinking and of interacting with others. It is a process that moves from visual perception to thoughts/beliefs, then to desire, and finally to action. First, there is the admiration of video models (guys like them, favorite Rappers like them). Next there is the desire to look like the video models (guys will desire me and people will think I'm pretty if I look like the video girls). Finally comes the process of changing hair, eyes, dress, attitude, thinking, and way of interacting with others.

The girls on Rap videos are sassy, sexy, bold, and sexually assertive. They know they are "bad" and they flaunt it. As previously discussed, girls and teens in general go through sexual development within an expected (expected because they are not grown-up yet) context of ignorance, uncertainty, and hormonal urges. During puberty, they are very vulnerable to media influences and to manipulation of their sexual energy. So when a 12- or 13-year-old girl begins to examine her physical beauty in comparison to those of Rap video models, problems develop. Possibly, the least of these problems is exhibiting a defiant attitude toward both peers and adults.

Before moving to more serious behaviors, let's take a further look at attitude. Adolescent and pre-adolescent girls, just like adolescent boys, are uncertain and insecure in regard to their bodies and their mental abilities. They know that they don't know very much about people and about life in general. They often feel that their bodies aren't pretty, and if they do believe their bodies are pretty, they are insecure and somewhat fearful about male attention to their bodies, though they use a sassy "front" to hide their insecurities. What we often have are young girls with adult bodies who give an appearance of being much more mature than they actually are. Their attitude can range from mild defiance or rebellion to extreme vulgarity and verbal aggression. Parents, peers, and teachers are often the targets of these negative attitudes.

Many African American parents find their pre-adolescent and adolescent daughters "getting beside themselves," meaning that these girls have begun to talk back to parents, "suck their teeth" at parents, come home past their curfew, talk to boys that parents have put off-limits, and wear clothes that parents have repeatedly instructed them not to wear. Understand: Rap video images contribute to a great deal of this. If unchecked, the behaviors of these young girls become worse.

If a young Black girl does not have an adult female to explain that her attitude and behaviors are not healthy and to set and enforce limits, the girl will probably self-destruct. She will take on somewhat of an exhibitionist persona, literally advertising her body. Her conversation will focus on subjects that directly relate to her mind-set, dress, and attitude: What the latest Rappers are recording and gossip about the Rappers' personal lives; the latest fashions; getting high; dating the finest guys or dating guys that drive nice cars; and her sexual activities.

In her misled, misdirected, programmed mind she has become a video model legend. Just like the women in the Rap videos, she, too, is now sexually attractive, pretty (as long as she keeps her hair long and blond, her eyes blue or green or hazel, and reveals as much of breasts, thighs, and buttocks as possible) and has lots of guys talking about her and desiring her. She is essentially lost. Almost any guy with a video or digital camera that wants pictures of her is given quick approval. These girls are often underage but will attend as many adult functions and Black college events as they can. They wear bikinis and act the part of *Girls Gone Wild*. She is a video model legend in her own mind.

Drinking a little alcohol, smoking a little weed, snorting a little coke, and popping a few ecstasy pills is only part of the party. She becomes a little bolder in the type of pictures she allows guys to take of her. This Black girl develops an open mind about sex and will begin to experiment with threesomes and with lesbian sex. It's only a party, after all. She's advanced in her thinking (a legend in her own mind), in her dress, and in her behaviors. Everyone else is square and so "old school." She develops a reputation that, initially, looks like a good one.

By the time she realizes that she is lost, there are several situations that exist or may exist, which are as follows: 1) She is now on several guys' videotapes (of a sexual nature) and has probably been viewed by many different people. 2) She has had numerous sexual partners, both male and female, and has been discussed among many different people. 3) She has developed a drug addiction. 4) She has had numerous abortions. 5) She has had several babies, usually by different men. 6) Academics have taken a back seat to her new lifestyle or have been abandoned altogether.

Before going further, I will make comments about mothers that contribute to thrusting their daughters into the midst of this madness. Too many Black mothers make the mistake of "being friends" with their daughters at the expense of being a parent who provides guidance and sets and enforces limits. Some of these mothers actually purchase the revealing clothes for their daughters and even wear such clothes themselves. They believe that they "are too young" to dress grown-up and seek every opportunity to place themselves in situations where someone is likely to say, "Y'all look like sisters instead of mother and daughter!"

Does Your Daughter Want To Be a "Video Ho"?

Tragically, some of these Black mothers even date (have sex with) males that are not that much older than their daughters. The daughter is sexing a "thug" and mama is in the next bedroom with her "thug." They meet these men when they go clubbing with their daughters. Things come to a head when daughter becomes pregnant or when one of their boyfriends attempts to have sex with both of them or when mother experiences some type of very embarrassing moment. The logic given by these mothers is foolish, immature, and twisted. These are often adult women who were never provided the kind of guidance during childhood that is necessary for helping them, in turn, to provide guidance to their children.

Whenever a female child or adolescent seeks to become a person whose *only* attributes are physical (i.e., breasts, behinds, face, hair length/color, legs), destruction may be close behind. In a society where young girls yearn to appear on shows such as *America's Next Top Model* and *Who Wants To Marry a Millionaire?* there are bound to be a great many lost children in that society. America is at the top of the heap. America manufactures childhood destruction via its popular culture. Media, entertainment, and fashion-industry values are not in line with healthy family values. Black folk, possibly more than any other group in the world, should not argue this reality. We pay three times the consequences, figuratively speaking, than Whites and others when we mess up.

One of the greatest challenges Blacks face in saving Black children is the influence of popular, well-loved Black entertainers who are extremely negative role models for Black youth. We don't know how to love them and confront them at the same time. But we better learn and we better learn fast! When becoming a successful Black entertainer comes at the expense of young Black minds, we have a real problem. Is it possible that the way to control Blacks and others is through a form of mind and value control brought to bear by the media/entertainment/fashion industry? Proof may be seen in the fact that many people in the Rap industry call video models *video hos.*

Proof of mind control/value control of Blacks may also be seen in the fact that Snoop Dogg, the most famous Rapper and a popular actor, has produced pornographic movies starring Black "actresses." Proof of mind control of Blacks may be seen in Mary J. Blige appearing to be running away from Blackness by wearing blond hair and blue or hazel contact lenses. Whenever the people who are idolized by children and youth exhibit and/or advocate unhealthy beliefs and lifestyles, the future of those idolators is placed in jeopardy. The children are the seeds of a people's future, and if the seeds are contaminated, then the people become poisoned and the future is canceled. We do not need any more Black girls seeking to become "video hos."

8. Player or Sexual Predator?

The current African American male image in popular culture is primarily that of "player" or "thug." Let's look at the dynamics of a Black male player and examine his *true* role in the lives of his people. I strongly encourage you to share this chapter with Black male children, Black male adolescents, and Black male adults and to discuss, debate, and argue this with them.

A player in the Black community is dangerous for a number of reasons. The very word "play" brings to mind that which is not serious and that which is, to a large extent, childish or child-like. The act of playing is associated with games; and people play games. Therefore, when a woman gets involved with a player, she has unknowingly become a participant in a game. She may be very serious about developing a relationship but does not know that he is only playing because his mind is child-like (although he believes he is mature).

The Black male player deceives the woman into believing he truly cares about her, that he loves her and wants to be with only her. He grooms the woman (gifts, attention, a fake show of caring) in order to get her to feel obligated to him and to make her emotionally comfortable. She (an unknowing victim) eventually falls for his "game." He sexes her until he gets his fill, then he starts "tripping": not returning her phone calls; being too busy to see her; being impatient when talking with her; and developing a negative attitude toward her. She may eventually hear that he is seeing another woman or other women. She becomes confused, hurt, and angry. She has been played.

The player produces lots of bitter women and single mothers. This will continue for a very, very long time because we have tens of thousands of 11, 12, and 13-year-old Black boys working very hard to become players, just like their favorite Rappers, some male family members, and older peers. Black boys hear lyrics and see Rap videos that brag about having lots of "hos" and lots of "bitches." Most Rappers don't rap about respecting Black women and strengthening Black communities. No, they rap about sexing Black females (the more the merrier), killing other Black men, purchasing expensive jewelry, purchasing expensive rims and cars, drinking expensive alcoholic beverages, and imitating Mafia gangsters. Rappers strongly promote the development of players in the Black community. It has gotten so bad, Brothers and Sisters, that many young Brothers are teased by peers if they are not sexing several girls. Destiny's Child, Missy Elliott, and other female singers/Rappers do not help matters when they record songs that place "hot boys" and "soldiers" and "thugs" on pedestals. These songs only encourage Black males to become Black-on-Black killers (thugs) and to expect that Black girls want them to be "hot boys," "thugs," and "soldiers" (soldiers fight an enemy; so who will these Brothers fight? They will fight and kill other Brothers).

Players or Sexual Predator?

We Black folk are caught up in a deadly cycle of player-production-player-perpetuation. During the European slave trade, Whites used Black males as breeders who were forced to have sex with Black women to produce babies (workers) for the plantation owner. Today we have players, but they are not forced to produce workers, they are simply programmed to facilitate the destruction of Black people. Understand: The sole purpose of a Black male player (he does not know this because he has no awareness) is to speed up the process of destroying Black people.

The Black male player is guilty of producing un-fathered children, who may end up on the new slave plantations called juvenile detention, jail, and prison. He may have several children by different women. The player spends no time raising and teaching and loving his children because he is too busy *playing* more *games* with other females. The Black male player prevents the development of *umoja* (unity) in the Black community because players engender the *distrust* and the *dislike* of all Black men. This Brother has unknowingly become an enemy of his people. Now, let's look at the player as sexual predator.

Players are sexual predators. Am I saying that they are sex offenders? Not in the legalistic sense but, yes, as relates to what they do they are *sexual predators*. A predator seeks out someone or something for the sole purpose of harming that person or animal. A predator does not seek to help his prey. The prey is the victim. The Black male player preys upon Black females; this means that he does something bad to them, something they would not want done to them.

Gail Ryan states:

> Sexually abusive behavior has been defined as any sexual interaction with person(s) of any age that is perpetrated (1) against the victim's will, (2) without consent, or (3) in an aggressive, exploitative, manipulative, or threatening manner. It may be characterized by one or more of a wide array of behaviors....

Let's look at the above quote. Do Black women willfully have sex with players? Yes, but it is not that simple. Do Black women consent to have sex with players? Yes, but this answer, too, is not that simple. Are players aggressive, exploitive, manipulative, or threatening in their preying upon Black women? To varying degrees, players are all of these. When a man deliberately seeks out a woman for the sole purpose of having sex with her, and the woman does not know that all this man wants is sex, and she would not even talk with this man if she knew his true intention, this is by its very nature a sexually predatory act. He is a predator of a sexual nature, and she is his prey or victim.

Gail Ryan further explains the relationship:

Players or Sexual Predator?

In any sexual interaction, the factors that are useful when assessing the presence or absence of exploitation are equality, consent, and coercion. *Equality* considers differentials of physical, cognitive, and emotional development, passivity and assertiveness, power and control, and authority....*Consent* considers agreement, including *all* of the following: (1) understanding what is proposed based on age, maturity, developmental level, functioning, and experience; (2) knowledge of societal standards for what is being proposed; (3) awareness of potential consequences and alternatives; (4) assumption that agreements or disagreements will be respected equally; (5) voluntary decision; [and] (6) mental competence.

Is the relationship between the player and his prey equal? No, because the player's emotional corruption and miseducation as relates to being a man has sunk him to a pathological, immoral level as relates to right and wrong. In the player's twisted logic, it is "right" to do this "wrong" (deceive a female into having sex with him). There is also no consent present when players approach and engage their victims; this is true because the element of deception is present. If a woman does not want to be a sexual toy but gives in to a man whom she believes respects her, cares for her, and wants to build a future with her, she is not consenting to his sex-only agenda.

Black boys, adolescents, and adult males who deliberately seek to deceive Black girls, teens, and adult females into having sex with them by way of fake caring, fake respect, and a fake show of love are sexual predators. They are having fun while simultaneously destroying Black families and communities by creating un-fathered children (who too often get into all sorts of trouble), emotionally wounded females, and distrust of all Black males.

Negative Rappers significantly contribute to instilling a "player" mind-set in Black boys. These destructive Rappers encourage Black boys to deceive, use, and disrespect Black girls. When these Black boys become adults, they continue the same destructive behavior toward Black women. Negative Rappers are encouraging Black boys to associate manhood with having sex with lots of females. Negative Rappers are helping to destroy their own people, and they do not know this. (I would like to think that if they knew the consequences, they would stop; if they do know but refuse to stop, then they don't care.)

If we can teach a generation of Black boys that being a player is deadly to Black families and to Black communities, and teach them to understand the emotional damage players do to women, we would be able to stop this madness. And when some of these properly educated boys become Rappers, they will be able to make their millions without degrading women and without poisoning the minds of other Black males.

"Folks don't even own themselves. Paying mental rent to corporate presidents."

—Public Enemy, from their song *He Got Game*

"Though it's thousands of miles away,
Sierra Leone connect to what we go through today.
Over here it's a drug trade; we die from drugs.
Over there, they die from what we buy from drugs.
The diamonds, the chains, the braces, the charms."

—Kanye West, from his song *Diamonds from Sierra Leone*

9. How Rappers Are Being Pimped

African American Rappers are pimped by White corporate America's fashion, jewelry, clothes (including sneakers), beverage (alcoholic beverages), automobile, and tobacco (Black & Mild, Swisher Sweets, White Owl, GPC, Blunts, etc.) industries. The fact that some Rappers imitate the pimps by establishing their own expensive name-brand clothes lines is irrelevant because imitation of one's oppressor/exploiter only serves to further the exploitation and oppression of the exploited Black child and adolescent who is already at or below the poverty line. Though many of us are proud that Black entertainers create their own fashion lines, we must know that the exploited are not empowered simply because a Black exploiter has joined a White exploiter. How many poor, inner-city Black youth are these Rappers employing through their product lines? How many Black youth are struggling to purchase Rappers' products that are just as expensive as Hilfiger and Polo?

Black Rappers do not own/control/operate/produce/manage diamond and gold mines or GMC, Toyota, Mercedes, Jaguar, Tommy Hilfiger, Phillip Morris, or anything else besides their own lines (and Whites manage these). Rappers are pimped by the people who do own, manufacture, operate, and control all the above businesses.

First, let's look at the pimp. A pimp is someone who has others earning money for him, with little or no benefit or profit going to the person(s) being pimped. The person being pimped has *hopes* and *dreams* that one day the pimp will end their drudgery and set them up in luxury and wealth. As revealed in their lyrics, many Rappers fantasize about unlimited money and power and influence. This is an expression of their hopes and dreams of one day being the next Bill Gates or Donald Trump or Al Capone or Al Pacino's fictitious Tony Montana from the movie *Scarface*.

Rappers have become human billboards and non-salaried advertisers for the alcohol, fashion, automobile, and jewelry industries. Their lyrics, videos, and lifestyle serve to whet the appetite of economically

How Rappers Are Being Pimped

poor Black youth for items they can't afford but will do almost anything to acquire. Secondly, these Rappers increase the profit margins of the industries that manufacture the items Rappers brag about owning. What drives this behavior? Many Rappers seek to personify the Black person who has obtained the American Dream. Through their lyrics and videos, many Rappers are essentially saying, "Hey, Black folk, look at me! I drive a Jaguar and a Lexus; I drink Cristal and Courvoisier; I have a platinum grill; I got dozens of outfits from every designer in existence; I wear a Rolex; I am a success!" Sadly, this madness will not stop any time soon.

Black Rappers are unknowingly caught in a manipulative ploy of life imitating art as art imitates life. Confusing? Let's examine this. Juliet Schor explains:

> Edgy style has associations with Rap and hip-hop, with "street" and African American culture. In the 1990s, ads aimed at white, middle-class Americans began to be filmed in inner-city neighborhoods with young Black men as the stars. The ads made subtle connections to violence, drugs, criminality, and sexuality—the distorted and stereotypical images of young Black men that have pervaded the mainstream media.

The environment of poverty and danger faced by many African Americans became a marketing tool for advertising to middle-class White Americans. Through the safety of media, ads depicting the hardships of White-supremacy-induced Black poverty allowed Whites to "experience" the uncertainty, stress, and dangers (called "edgy" by corporate America) of being Black in America. Juliet Schor goes on to explain:

> The story of how street [culture] came to be at the core of consumer marketing began more that 30 years ago…[with] the practice of athletic shoe companies, starting with Converse in the late 1960s and, more recently, Nike and its competitors. The shoe manufacturers intentionally associated their product with African American athletes, giving free shoes to coaches in the inner cities, targeting inner-city consumers in their research, attaching their brand to street athletics and sociability.

Positive rap group Public Enemy wrote a song entitled *Politics of the Sneaker Pimps*. They were absolutely correct in their description of the athletic shoe company as sneaker pimps, regarding their exploitation of Black male youth and pimping of Black athletes. These sneaker companies were among the first to begin pimping high-profile Blacks and the Black

How Rappers Are Being Pimped

community in general (remember, if someone we look up to does or wears something, then we are likely to see it as OK and desirable). Schor explains, in the above quote, that these shoe manufacturers attached "sociability" to their brands. What "sociability" means is that Black inner-city youth will view themselves as someone important, valued, and worthwhile if they own a certain brand of sneakers. Certain sneakers became associated with one's social standing among peers and one's self-esteem and self-image. This is a killer in Black communities across America. Several years ago, while visiting Brooklyn for a book signing/lecture, I was invited to attend a rally in the Bronx. The purpose of the rally was to garner support for a protest of sneaker companies because two Black youth were murdered for their Jordans.

Clothing manufacturers got into this lucrative act, too. Schor writes:

> Apparel companies, beginning with Tommy Hilfiger, became active in this world, giving rap stars and other prominent taste-makers free samples of their latest styles.

Rappers wear expensive designer clothes, brag about this in their lyrics, and show them in their videos. Black children and adolescents, eager to fit in, waste no time nagging mother (those with both parents will nag father, too) or grandmother or whomever the caretaker is, to purchase these name-brand items. Many Black parents find themselves deciding between a utility bill or a Sean Jean outfit. Too many Black youth are afraid of being teased by peers because they only have one pair of Jordans or because their clothes aren't name brand (e.g., "Yo, niggah, you ain't got no name-brand clothes!" "Man, all your sh** comes from Wal Mart."). Books and academics often take a back seat to clothing, jewelry, and sneakers. It breaks my heart that some of our children wear $500 worth of stuff to school but would not carry one book and is behind in grade level.

The child being teased eventually ends up contributing to the profit margins of White and Asian businesses. With the help of Rappers, Black children are literally pressuring each other into making other people rich. When Sean Combs or 50 Cent or Jay Z rap about wealth and reinforce their lyrics through videos showing clothes, jewelry, cars, and half-naked females to an audience of Black adolescents, they are encouraging their own people to worry/misspend/over-spend/sell drugs/shoplift/mis-prioritize in their efforts to achieve the American Dream.

Rappers also place a lot of pressure on Black children and teens to drink alcoholic beverages and to smoke cigarettes and marijuana. The words "chronic," "weed," "indo," "blunt," "sess," and others are popular with many Black male and female teens. Dr. Dre, Ice Cube (especially in his *Friday* movies), Snoop Dogg (especially Snoop's *Gin & Juice* hit), and most other

How Rappers Are Being Pimped

Rappers have glamorized smoking marijuana to a maddening level. These Brothers do not know that marijuana and alcohol are gateway drugs; the two drugs that are likely to lead to cocaine (crack), heroin, and other drug use. Thus far in my counseling career, I have not worked with one crack addict who did not start getting high with weed and alcohol. I wish I knew how many Rappers are drug addicts (addicted to alcohol or marijuana or crack or ecstasy or heroin). If any of them are, they should start traveling across the country warning Black youth not to associate being "down" with getting high.

It is has gotten so bad that many Black youth *believe* that they are *supposed* to act a certain way not only around their peers but *especially in public*. Juliet Schor, quoting Douglas Rushkoff, writes:

> It's turned into a giant feedback loop: you watch kids to find out what trend is "in," but the kids are watching you watching them in order to figure out how to act. They are exhibitionists, aware of corporate America's fascination with their every move, and delighting in your obsession with their tastes.

Right after the above quote, Schor states that, "Although there's a democratic veneer to the feedback loop, that perspective obscures the fact that giant businesses orchestrate, control, and profit from the process." The fact that corporate America will exploit anyone, to some extent, should be no consolation to African Americans. Corporate America is run by White men with racial views and philosophies that often place Blacks in a category with animals, just as we were during chattel slavery. They have no love for the Rappers they pimp into persuading us to become the ultimate consumers, and hey undoubtedly view Rappers as jokes, clowns, and buffoons seeking to imitate White gangsters and White businessmen.

"Minds on vacation"
—Public Enemy, from their song *Unstoppable*

"Crowd goin' crazy. Gettin' bigger. Proud to be called a bunch of b*****s and niggas."
—Public Enemy, from their song *Is Your God a Dog?*

10. Where Y'all At?: Positive Rappers Search for a Black Audience

We got a problem, Brothers and Sisters. Black youth are droppin' it like it's hot and glorifying Glocks while White youth are attending the concerts of such positive Black Rappers as Public Enemy, KRS-One, Zion-I, The Coup, and others. Those most in need of the messages given by positive Rappers are not attending their concerts and are undoubtedly not buying their CDs. When it comes to reaching and teaching their Brothers and Sisters, positive Black Rappers are attempting to swim up waterfalls.

Bakari Kitwana writes:

> Armed with messages of Black political resistance, Black pride, and opposition to militarization and corporatization, designed in part to counter the commercial hip-hop-party-and-bullsh** madness dumbing down the nation's youth, hip-hop's lyrical descendants

of the "fight the power" golden era today are booking concerts in record numbers—far beyond anything imaginable by their predecessors. Problem is, they can hardly find a Black face in the audience.

The article also mentions the fact that blues and jazz have become the choice of a mostly Caucasian audience. We are in trouble. When the children of one's oppressor finds meaning and/or entertainment in the lyrics of conscious African American artists while the children of the oppressed find delight in vulgar, sexually explicit, violence-laden lyrics, it reeks of the Biblical last days—but only for the oppressed. What dynamics are taking place here? Let's look at several.

First, Bakari Kitwana, explaining that there was not a significant gap between the hip-hop artists' generation and the civil rights generation during the 1980s, mentioned the CD jacket on Public Enemy's 1990 *Fear of a Black Planet*. Kitwana explained that the CD's lyrics were within the reality of the civil rights movement. There was no disconnect; the Black artist and the Black politician/masses shared a common understanding of their common problem, which was and still is White supremacy (racism). Kitwana explained that Public Enemy's CD "extensively quoted" Frances Cress Welsing's "Cress Theory of Color Confrontation." Bakari Kitwana writes:

Where Ya'll At? Positive Rappers Search for a Black Voice.

Welsing also had another, less-known theory, regarding the inferiorization of Black children. Welsing argued that soon White supremacists wouldn't have to worry about making Blacks seem inferior—they'd just need to keep providing them with inferior education, housing, health care, child care, and the like, and in a generation or two they would be. After 15 years of gangstas and bling, perhaps hip-hop's Black audience has been so inundated with material garbage that they don't want an uplifting message.

Black youth; along with all Blacks, have been deliberately miseducated, misinformed, and misled in American society, and as a result are now self-destructive. Knowledge of self is necessary to counter and to prevent this self-destruction, but when one's oppressor facilitates the destruction of the Black family and then is given the opportunity to educate the children of the oppressed, these children will never receive knowledge of self. Remember, Elijah Muhammad stated that if a man does not treat you right, he won't teach you right. This creates a lose-lose situation. Blacks lose. The so-called integration of Blacks into American society gave civil rights-era Blacks illusions of progress because laws changed and token symbols of progress appeared. However, we now know that laws don't change hearts; they only force those historically opposed to those laws to revert to institutional, hidden racism (White supremacy).

Am I blaming Blacks, who fought and died for us to obtain civil rights, for today's Black youth calling themselves b*****s and hos? No. I am agreeing with Harry Belafonte's statement that Dr. Martin Luther King, Jr., feared that Blacks were being integrated into a house that is morally on fire. In other words, we were not prepared for the type of morality that existed in the collective White community. We Black folk thrive within the spirit/mentality/behavior of cooperation, sharing, and living an "our"-"us"-"we" lifestyle, wrapped within a spiritual covering. We underestimated the destructive moral consequences of immersing ourselves in White values, beliefs, and behaviors.

The White controlled-owned-operated electronic and print media, the fashion industry, and some members of White society's disrespect for God's Word (i.e., prayer is taken out of school and Ritalin is put in school; men are allowed to marry men and women are allowed to marry women; billions are spent to seduce kids into smoking and drinking) have lured Black youth into a lustful, sexually confused/sexually charged belief and value system in which jewelry, cars, clothes, marijuana, sex, guns, and sneakers are more important than anything Public Enemy, Brand Nubian, KRS-One, Poor Righteous Teachers, or The Coup could rap about. These things have become nothing less than a form of crack cocaine for Black youth.

Where Ya'll At? Positive Rappers Search for a Black Voice.

More powerful than the "15 years of gangstas and bling" that Kitwana spoke of is the influence of White supremacy on the formation of Black minds and behaviors because it is White supremacy that created and glorified outlaws, gangsters, and their murderous exploits, primarily through Hollywood movies and television in general. Al Capone acquired wealth through crime, as did the fictional Tony Montana from the movie *Scarface*. Many Black male youth, miseducated about manhood and Black history and frustrated by White supremacy's economic system, began to identify with White gangsters instead of with Jesse Jackson or Johnnie Cochran or Al Sharpton or the neighborhood guy who cooks or drives a bus to provide for his wife and kids.

The lesson of Malcolm X (redemption through knowledge of self) is rapidly and thoroughly being displaced by a "Get Rich or Die Trying" mentality. Many Black and Latino male youth, with tremendous help from this racist society and the negative Rappers that help White supremacy, have become experts at the following: 1) killing each other; 2) making jewelry store owners wealthy; 3) impregnating females but not accepting the responsibility of fatherhood; 4) making auto accessory stores wealthy (buying rims); 5) making coffin manufacturers wealthy (through killing each other); 6) making gun manufacturers wealthy (through purchasing guns illegally, but purchasing them none the less); 7) making sneaker manufacturers wealthy

(Jawanza Kunjufu explained that Nike manufactures sneakers for $2.38; Brothers and Sister pay more that $100 for some Jordans); and 8) contributing to the new slave plantation called the prison-industrial complex. So, who's listening to positive Rappers?

White youth. "My audience has gone from being over 95 percent Black 10 years ago to over 95 percent White today," laments Boots Riley of the Coup, whose 1994 *Genocide and Juice* responded to Snoop Dogg's 1993 gangsta party anthem, *Gin and Juice*. (Kitwana, 2005) When I look at it, I am reminded that politically conscious Reggae artists also have majority White audiences. Black youth purchase Bob Marley tee-shirts but not his music. They relate to smoking weed but not to Bob's politically conscious messages. Whites purchase the music, even though they, too, smoke weed. Kitwana writes:

> Zion, who believes the withering Black audience reflects the diminishing discussion of Blackness in public discourse, thinks that Black youth have been inundated with material garbage. "I do so many shows in front of mostly white audiences that it's the norm," says Zion. "When I get in front of a Black audience it's like, 'Finally you're here, feel me.' We've done shows in Chicago and Sao Paulo, Brazil, and it feels good to be in front of our people when

Where Ya'll At? Positive Rappers Search for a Black Voice.

they are feeling it. But there are some thugged-out crowds where our message doesn't resonate, and Black folks will say that they aren't trying to hear hip-hop artists remind them of their problems."

The artist, Zion, interviewed by Bakari Kitwana, stated that the "diminishing discussion of Blackness in public discourse" is a major cause of Black youth not being into politically conscious rap. Zion went on to state that some Black youth are too "thugged-out" to listen to conscientious rap, while others "aren't trying to hear hip-hop artists remind them of their problems." If Blacks are running from Blackness (which in some ways resembles a psychosis, which is detachment from reality), then many White youth are running to Blackness, even though they are not giving up White supremacist beliefs and values. However, they are more in tune with political discourse (i.e., President Bush; the Iraq war; pollution; effects of globalization) and enjoy artists that stimulate their minds and provide encouragement for them to continue along a given path. This is what Black conscientious Rappers do for Whites.

Kitwana states:

Today's climate is indeed a far cry from the African medallion mania of the 1980s. In the

85

academy, we've gone from 1980s discussions of Black studies and Afrocentricity to multi-culturalism to current-day debates about post-Blackness and polyculturalism. At the same time, in the arena of mainstream politics we've gone from discussing the collective Black impact of Jesse Jackson's run for president to the individual career successes of Clarence Thomas, Colin Powell, and Condoleezza Rice. In the streets we've gone from the Nation of Islam patrolling housing projects to Whites reclaiming Harlem, South Side Chicago, and East Oakland and Black scholars like Columbia University's Lance Freeman arguing that poor Blacks aren't significantly displaced by gentrification.

Clearly, Black America has gotten way off track. We have been deceived into ignoring and running away from ourselves. We are now a colonized people living within the illusion of White acceptance. Is the rap music industry, which is overwhelmingly negative, serving to colonize Black America?

Norman Kelley in a 1999 article entitled "The Political Economy of Black Music" wrote:

The six major record firms have a colonial-like relationship with the Black Rhythm Nation of America that produces hip-hop and other

Where Ya'll At? Positive Rappers Search for a Black Voice.

forms of Black music. Despite the names of a few big money makers—Suge Knight, Sean Combs, and Russell Simmons—or the lurid deaths of Tupac Shakur and Christopher Wallace (also known as…Biggie Smalls), rap, like most Black music, is under the corporate control of whites….

What exists is a neo-slavery condition in which some Blacks are "allowed" to make money as long as they stay within the realm of operation allowed by White corporations. If rap is a "game," then Blacks have lost the game. Think about it. Who benefited from an East Coast-West Coast rivalry? The major record companies owned by Whites. Black Rappers are being used like gladiators in a Roman coliseum, and they fight each other to the death to the amusement and profit of White corporate "Caesars." The White men in suits don't have to shoot each other or call White women b*****s and hos in order to "get paid"; they simply pay some Black Rappers to do it for them.

This amounts to musical genocide, which is nothing more than disseminating funky beats with destructive lyrics that are intended to affect and effect a specific population very differently from other listeners. For example, suburban Whites and inner-city Blacks both listen to negative rap, but Whites have not been miseducated and socialized to hate themselves and have not, as a group, been frustrated economically. White society provides a safety net for Whites. So, even though both listen to the same songs, it is the Black youth who begin to imitate White gangsters (real or imagined); it is the Black youth who sell crack cocaine on street corners; it is the Black youth who purchase illegal handguns (White America has millions of legal handguns).

Here's a crude analogy: If you have an infestation of ants and roaches in your home and you use ant spray to get rid of them, you will be disappointed when you find out that the spray made to kill ants does not kill roaches. It is the same with musical genocide.

Norman Kelley goes on to state:

> The relationship between Black music and the "Big Six" is a post-modern form of colonialism…. Products were produced in a "raw periphery" and sent back to the imperial "motherland" to be finished into commodities, sold in the metropolitan centers or back to the colonies, with the result being that the colony's economic growth was stunted because it was denied its ability to engage in manufacturing products for its own needs and exports. With Rap, the inner cities have become the raw sites of "cultural production" and the music then

Where Ya'll At? Positive Rappers Search for a Black Voice.

sold to the suburbs, to White youths who claim they can "relate" to those of the urban bantustans.

Kelley paints a disturbing picture of the Rap industry. All across America there are tens of thousands of Black boys and girls desiring and working feverishly to become the next big Rapper. And the White owned and operated record companies are waiting on them. With the promise of a dozen cars and all the bling they can handle, our children are transformed into colonized Frankenstein creations that embark on a vulgar journey of advocating sexual promiscuity, drug use, violence, and blind consumerism.

There are other Black Rappers that also carry positive messages, though not often of a political nature. These are our Christian Rappers. Though some people have mixed views of Christian Rappers (e.g., "rap music is not gospel music," "people shouldn't be dancing to gospel music," "this can lead children to that *other* Rap music," etc.), I have come to the conclusion that it is better for Black 13-, 14-, 15-, 16-, and 17-year-olds to listen to Holy Hustlas' record artists Kirk Franklin, Terrance Bailey, Victorius, and a host of other Christian Rappers than to Snoop Dogg, Scarface, 50 Cent, and other Black Rappers that are helping their Brothers and Sisters to self-destruct. Would you rather hear your child singing a Rap song about Jesus The Christ or about Glock handguns, smoking weed, and having sex? To save our children and ourselves, we must develop and utilize life-enhancing alternatives to gangster Rap.

"Men provide for their family; protect their family; and defend their family."

—Frances Cress Welsing, M.D.

11. Rap and Manhood Development

First, a story.

Ms. Sadie Booker, 69 years old, puts on her hand-quilted sweater, picks up her walking stick, and prepares to leave her modest, two-bedroom home, of which she is extremely proud, to head to the bus stop, which is a half block away. As she closes her door, she makes sure to check to see that it is locked. She does not want another break in. The last break in cost her $235, which was the total cost for the television, kitchenware, and clothes she purchased from Wal-Mart. Slowly walking down the stairs as she exits her home, she glances up across the street at EJ, Lil Mack, and Ms. Coney's grandson, whose name she can't recall.

The three boys, all teenagers, are sitting on the steps of Lil Mack's home, drinking very large cans of beer. None of them speak to Ms. Sadie. She wonders why these boys have so many people visiting them for such short periods of time; they never stay more than two or three minutes. And the three boys are always dressed in new clothes; which makes Ms. Sadie wonder, since she can't figure out when they go to work or to school. As she takes a slow yet steady stroll to the bus stop, Ms. Sadie experiences a verbal attack: "All b*****s

91

suck d*ck! All niggers eat p***y!" The song is coming from a passing car and can be heard blocks away. After all these years, Ms. Sadie has not gotten used to the profanity these young people listen to.

Yards away from the bus stop, Ms. Sadie sees two young men sitting on the bench at the stop. They are talking and eating fast food. When Ms. Sadie stops, she hears one of the young men giggling, as he says to his friend, "Sh**, niggah, you get yo a** up and let her sit down! I'm just like Rosa Parks!" After they toss their trash onto the ground, the talker's friend gets up and allows Ms. Sadie to take his seat.

Boarding the bus and taking a seat, Ms. Sadie looks out the window, as her mind begins to drift. Looking at the houses and the people, she remembers when the neighborhood was clean and the people took so much pride in owning their homes. She remembers when there were no trash cans at bus stops and no trash was thrown onto the street. Ms. Sadie remembers when children would not dare to cuss around grown folk and would get up in a flash when an adult female or old person didn't have a seat. She remembers when songs didn't call females b*****s and hos and didn't have any cussing in them. She remembers and she cries. It is a soft cry, with tears rolling down her face in slow motion. The End.

    Do most Rappers rap about or exemplify Black men that provide for their family, protect their family, and defend their family? No. Do most Rappers encourage Black males to respect Black females? No. Do most Rappers encourage Black people to own, operate, and control their own businesses (other than the destructive crack-cocaine dealing "business")? No. Do most Rappers rap about and encourage Black youth to respect the elderly and to treat the neighborhood in which they live with respect? No. Then what is it that most Rappers do?

Most Rappers are negative Rappers. Most Rappers, through their lyrics, videos, and lifestyle, encourage Black youth to have sex. Most Rappers encourage Black youth to purchase only name-brand clothes. Most Rappers encourage Black youth to kill other Blacks. Most Rappers encourage Black youth to purchase lots of expensive jewelry. Most Rappers encourage Black youth to purchase cars and expensive rims. Most Rappers, through their lyrics, videos, and lifestyle, encourage Black youth to smoke marijuana and to drink malt liquor and liquor. So, are Rappers helping to develop caring, conscientious, competent Black men? No.

We, the African American community, are in dire need of caring, conscientious, competent Black men to serve our families and communities. Negative Rappers are lending a helping hand to the owners of funeral parlors, casket companies, gun companies, jails, and prisons. They are not helping to save us but are assisting in developing a mind-set and behavior that helps Black youth become inmates instead of caring, conscientious, competent helpers of the African Village. The Rapper's cry for Black youth to become gangsters, pimps, players, and thugs is guaranteed to help keep Black America at the bottom of the socioeconomic ladder. With thousands of Black boys desiring and attempting to become the next Nelly, Lil Wayne, Scarface, 50 Cent, Snoop Dogg, and Three 6 Mafia, does the Black community stand a chance of surviving?

It is tragic that Blacks have been oppressed and programmed and miseducated to the extent that our young people are assisting in destroying themselves and, hence, our future. Pavlov and Skinner could not have done a better job with dogs and rats in conditioning a community to self-destruct. Destroying a people by way of their entertainment is genius! The victims actually run to their destruction, seeking fun, on a daily basis while simultaneously destroying themselves.

Negative Rappers, via their lyrics, videos, and lifestyles, do nothing to help Black people. In a time when juvenile detention centers, jails, and prisons have become the new slave plantations for Blacks, the stakes are too high for us to simply see these Rappers as harmless entertainers. They are definitely not harmless, and I question whether or not they are truly entertainers.

Rap and Manhood Development

Whenever entertainment becomes synonymous with destruction in real life, it is *warfare*, not entertainment. Due to no knowledge of self and due to the blinding effect of money and fame, no matter how fleeting, Rappers are waging war on their own people. *Their people* are the b*****s, hos, and niggers that they rap about sexually degrading and killing.

On page 29 of the July 2005 issue of *Vibe* magazine, James Ragin III of Jacksonville, Florida, wrote this to the editors:

> Heaven help us. Was the question on your May 2005 cover, "Hip Hop Murders: Why Haven't We Learned Anything?" aimed at *Vibe* readers or its editors? Was it supposed to be thought provoking or just attention grabbing? I ask because *Vibe* glorified 50 Cent as Scarface on its April cover. The movie *Scarface* has been treated by the hip-hop community as a how-to manual to obtain the American Dream. You may be guilty of: 1) not doing your homework; 2) being hypocrites; and 3) promoting violence that the question on the cover rhetorically seeks to end. *Vibe* gets an F.

This Brother is on point.

We must first understand what Amos N. Wilson explained in *Black on Black Violence: Black Self Annihilation in Service of White Domination*. Wilson explained that inside the minds of Black male criminals (thugs and so-called gangsters) are images of White male gangsters, and the Brothers are imitating the heartless and murderous behaviors of these White men when they kill and maim Black men, women, and children. 50 Cent was imitating Al Pacino, as Pacino pretended to be a fictional person. Do you understand the madness in imitating an imitation?

America does not cultivate spiritual manhood or cooperative manhood or caring manhood. The African nature of Black people in America demands that we have spiritual, cooperative, caring men. What America develops and cultivates is a John Wayne-Al Capone-Jesse James-Billy the Kid-Clint Eastwood-Sylvester Stallone-Arnold Schwartzenegger-James Bond-John Dillinger manhood, which, in reality, is a callous, murderous, and ungodly manhood. This is what Blacks face: a male socialization process that socializes boys to be aggressive, insensitive killers. Toy guns to "pretend" kill in childhood; movies to glorify killing as a form of feel-good entertainment; the feeling of power that comes from having a gun in hand; and, finally, the act of killing—killing as a problem solver. Killing within the psychopathic logic of being God. This is the environment in which America's boys become men.

One industry that benefits from the conditioning that negative Rap lyrics, videos, and personalities have on Black youth is the prison industry. I remember sitting in a sentencing hearing in federal court. Jail inmates went one by one before a very tough White judge. I noticed that when the judge explained the fines the inmates would have to pay while incarcerated (about $25 per quarter), he would use the words "prison industry." Then, about an hour later, he said the word, "Unicor." After court I went to my computer to look up Unicor. I found out that Unicor is the trade name for Federal Prison Industries, Incorporated, which is based in Washington, D.C. This, Brothers and Sisters, is one of several reasons why we should call juvenile detention centers, jails, and prisons the new slave plantations. Rappers who encourage poor, miseducated Black boys and girls to lust for jewelry, cars, and expensive clothes and to become sexualized to the point of committing sexual offenses are helping an already racist social-economic system to enslave (incarcerate) Black people.

We need Black men in our communities. We need men who believe it wrong to call Black females b*****s, hos, hood rats, and freaks. We need men who will be embarrassed to cuss around others, especially their women. We need men who are able to teach Black boys by example. We need men who will inform little Black girls that they should not reveal their body to males by wearing suggestive fashions. We need Black men that open businesses in our communities and in others' communities. We need men whose presence makes women, children, and the elderly feel safe and secure. All of this, Brothers and Sisters, is what Black communities need. Ms. Sadie Booker would be happy to see some real Black men in her neighborhood. Her tears would then become tears of joy.

12. Rap and Womanhood Development

Suppose that five years from now there were no Black females or Black women but only b*****s, hos, hood rats, bait, skeezers, and freaks. You think this is too ridiculous to even imagine? Well know this: Enslaved Africans would have believed it to be ridiculous for us to *enjoy* calling each other "nigger." Things do change for the worse. Do you know who would be the ones most likely to call Black females the derogatory names mentioned above? Black females themselves. The popularity and magnetic effect of negative Rap on the perceptions, emotions, beliefs, and behaviors of Black female (as well as male) children may very well lead to redefining womanhood as we know it.

Rap-based womanhood is really no womanhood at all but only the condition of being frozen in a state of adolescent pathology. Imagine Lil Kim at 35, 40, and 45 years of age. Imagine Khia (of *My Neck, My Back* fame) at 35, 40, and 45 years of age. Will Missy Elliott call herself the "baddest b****" when she is 40 or 45 years old? If they do not change to caring, conscientious, competent Black women, they would simply be frozen in a state of adolescent pathology.

Black womanhood has been under attack ever since we were cast into the holds of slave ships to be brought over to America. What is happening now is a psychological warfare strategy to get the enemy (Blacks) to think in a manner that leads them to destroy themselves. Negative male and female Rappers may be corporate America's gangsters paid to assist in the destructive programming of their Black Brothers and Sisters. The Rappers lack of self-knowledge coupled with monetary incentives (which they hurriedly give to White auto dealers, White and Asian jewelers, White fine department stores, and White realtors) are prime ingredients that make certain she/he will not stop for one second in programming young girls to become what the Rappers are: madness in motion.

Young Black girls that grow from teens to twenties to thirties with negative female Rappers as their models for how to live, will end up as some combination of the following: 1) Single mothers; 2) Drug addicted; 3) In deep financial debt; 4) Incarcerated (acting like the female versions of male thugs); 5) Emotionally bitter and resentful; 6) Unemployed or underemployed; 7) Going from one emotionally and physically abusive relationship to another. Don't naively think that the majority of young Black girls will simply "grow out of it" and become caring, conscientious, competent Black women after internalizing the crazy philosophies, messages, and behaviors of negative female Rappers.

Negative Rap influence in the lives of Black girls assists the media (TV, movies) and fashion industries in convincing girls that their bodies are the most important thing about them. They are only face, breasts, hips, thighs, vaginas, and behinds—nothing more. Since they are only meat, they must utilize these body parts to make money and to achieve social status. When young Black girls hear the lyrics to Beyonce's song *Check On It*, and then view the video, the belief that their bodies are all they have is further emphasized. Can we expect a decrease in HIV/AIDS with this occurring in Black communities? No. Can we expect a decrease in sexual offenses against females with this occurring in Black communities? No. Can we expect a decrease in teen pregnancies and abortions with this occurring in Black communities? No.

There is an ocean of difference between how Lauryn Hill and Lil Kim can influence a Black girl. One encourages knowledge of self, self-respect, and positive growth while the other encourages disrespect of self, drug use, and violence. This matters and should never be taken lightly. The negative Rappers will always get the most air time on radio and television because the White power structure does not want conscientious, committed, competent Black women and men; they want self-destructive clowns and buffoons. We are not likely to see Lauryn Hill, India Arie, Sister Souljah, and Alicia Keys as much as we see and hear Rappers that deliver their own people into the jaws of menticide and death. Negative Rap is an enemy of womanhood development.

Negative Rap does not help a female to cultivate her inner beauty. As a matter of fact, negative Rap erases the concept and reality of inner beauty. Negative rap does not help a female to embark upon academic pursuits; she is only encouraged to use her body and to think in a scandalous manner in order to get the material things she wants. Negative Rap does not help females to establish healthy standards for accepting a mate; she is encouraged only to go for the guy with the money (to prostitute herself). Negative Rap does not help females to become good mothers; even with children, they will continue to live a very unhealthy lifestyle, thus providing unhealthy models for their children. Negative Rap lyrics, videos, and personalities serve only to assist in the mental, spiritual, and physical destruction of Black females.

13. Recommendations

I strongly recommend that each of the following groups discussed below (churches, parents, sororities, fraternities, etc.) conduct strategical, goal-oriented, unapologetic writing campaigns to the Congressional Black Caucus (we want their support) and more demanding, uncompromising letters to those companies that are seducing and poisoning our children, such as Viacom (they own BET), Sony/BMG, Universal, and Warner. On page 72 of Jawanza Kunjufu's *Hip-Hop Street Curriculum: Keeping It Real*, he lists names and addresses of these entities and more.

A nationally coordinated campaign would be wonderful. Maybe some people such as Tom Joyner and Steve Harvey would be willing to help; I believe Joyner and Harvey know the dangerous results of violent Rap lyrics that also advocate sexual promiscuity and drug and alcohol use among Black and Latino youth.

Hip-Hop Street Curriculum: Keeping It Real lists more than 100 easy-to-use, real-life activities that are excellent for conducting groups, classes, and rap sessions to help our teens and children develop understanding and life-enhancing beliefs and values. If you or your organization is uncertain about how to structure and conduct activities (other than sports) for our children, please check out from the public library or borrow or purchase a copy of *Hip-Hop Street Curriculum: Keeping It Real.*

As a Licensed Professional Counselor and a Juvenile Sex Offender Certified Counselor, I know that holding group talk sessions with children and teens allows the opportunity to help them understand how things affect them, and this opens the door for equipping them with new understanding and improved behavior. I believe in direct, hands-on approaches to helping teens; this helps them to understand the errors of their beliefs, and when they understand their thinking errors, most will make positive changes.

The African American Church

Black ministers must take on a more socially active role in helping to prevent the destruction of Black people. If there are 500 Black churches in a city, as many of them as possible should join together to do two things: 1) Conduct a series of "teaching sermons" on the dangers of *negative Rap*, not all Rap. These periodic sermons should be done simultaneously (i.e., 375 churches delivering the same message on the same day); this helps to develop conversation and interest among an entire city about how we must prevent our children from falling victim to negative Rap. 2) The Black church must hold talk groups with our youth, both those that attend the church and those from the community. Black youth must hear and see Black adults complain about sexually charged, violent, vulgar Rap and must have the experience of Black adults teaching them how to avoid this destruction. Black ministers must have the vision and courage to do this. Churches should also sponsor youth events designed to show our kids that they can have fun and dance without profanity-saturated lyrics and without violence-filled songs. It is important to offer alternatives to the negative Rap that our children have been programmed to enjoy and seek out. These alternatives are a way to deprogram our children.

African American Parents

African American parents must first talk with their children about the dangers of violent, sexually charged, vulgar Rap songs, videos, and personalities. Turn the TV, cell phones, and stereos off, sit down, and talk with your children. Let them know that negative Rap can influence many kids to smoke marijuana, drink alcohol, have sex, and commit violent acts. Let them know that too many kids try to imitate Rappers. Your children must be told, by you, that you love them too much to sit by and let their ears, eyes, and minds become filled with deadly songs and videos.

When your children say, "It's just a song" or "It's just a video," tell them they are incorrect because these vulgar, violent, sexually charged songs and videos influence too many youth to do bad things, and you do not take it lightly.

Second, Black parents must not purchase music that contains vulgar, violent, sexually charged lyrics and must put such music off-limits to the home. Will the children still listen to it somewhere else? They probably will, but setting and enforcing limits on this music is likely to make them think about what they are listening to in a more discerning (conscious) manner. Talking with your children about this can help your child develop insight into how these songs and videos influence kids. Be consistent in all of the above; when parents are consistent, their children take them seriously. Kids often last longer than parents because parents give in; then the child does whatever he or she wishes.

Should parents simply not include BET in their cable selection? For children and teens with any combination of a history of bad judgment, aggression, being overly impatient, failing grades, having a negative self-image (how they see themselves), easily giving in to peer pressure, and having low self-esteem (how they view their capabilities), I do not recommend BET or any cable station showing the kinds of videos shown on BET. Black Entertainment Television does more harm than good to the Black community. Negative Rap videos that glamorize sex, partying, getting high, and gun violence can lead these kids into the abyss.

Likewise for Black kids living in poverty, I do not recommend (though they may view these videos more frequently than others) BET or any television

106

station that shows videos similar to those on BET. Most Rap videos only whet the appetite of young Black boys and girls for jewelry, cars, name-brand clothes, guns, and sex. These videos and songs also influence children's attitudes toward parents, teachers, and other authority figures in a very negative, even hostile, way because negative Rappers project hostile, angry attitudes.

When you consider allowing your child to attend a teen event, include in your "what I expect" lecture the possibility that if you find out the event plays vulgar, violent, sexually charged songs, you may change your mind about letting them attend. There will be some parent-child stress over all of the above, but if you give in and allow BET, the streets, and peers to raise your child, then your child is doomed.

African American Sororities and Fraternities

Getting the sororities and fraternities that are present on university campuses to confront negative Rap may be difficult because too many of them have been programmed to accept and enjoy this destructive entertainment. However, those fraternity and sorority members that are mature and aware of how negative Rap influences Black youth can do a great deal to help. First, Black sororities and fraternities should hold talk groups to discuss reasons why Black youth should avoid negative Rap (the activities in *Hip-Hop Street Curriculum: Keeping It Real* are an excellent resource for this). These talk groups should be held both in the community and on college campuses.

Second, our sororities and fraternities should team up with Black churches and help these churches develop healthy programs and activities for Black youth. After discussing the dangerous influence of negative Rap on the thoughts and behaviors of Black youth, we must next provide as many alternative activities as possible (e.g., dances at which no profane Rap is played; cookouts; plays). Many Black youth hold fraternities and sororities in high esteem; therefore, these organizations can have significant positive impact on our youth.

Public Schools

Visionary, courageous public school principals, teachers, and superintendents should develop and implement an addendum to the curriculum that teaches the dangerous influence of vulgar, violent, sexually charged Rap songs, videos, and personalities on youth's beliefs and behaviors (again, *Hip-Hop Street Curriculum: Keeping It Real* would be excellent for this). Most students will say that Rap and Rappers don't influence them. They must be asked, "If 50 Cent, Snoop Dogg, Nelly, Ludacris, and others began to wear their pants up around their waste with a belt, what would other kids start doing?" Since public schools have a captive audience (children must attend by law), there is a tremendous opportunity to help save kids from the destructive influence of negative Rap songs and personalities.

Public schools can also bring in lecturers and speakers, both local and national figures. There are many conscientious, competent Black men and women in every Black community who are willing to go to schools and talk with youth. Principals must not be afraid to bring in a member of the Nation of Islam to address this problem. Whether public schools bring in Jawanza Kunjufu or Na'im Akbar or the conscientious Brother and Sister that live right across the street from the school, they should bring in someone. If public schools do this, they will help prevent everything from suspensions to drop-outs to killings.

Black Elected Officials and the National Association for the Advancement of Colored People (NAACP)

Black elected officials and the NAACP should meet with Black ministers, Black sororities and fraternities, and Black parents to hold local and national press conferences expressing their dislike and disappointment with negative Rappers, radio stations that play negative Rap, Black Entertainment Television (or is it Black Eroticizing Television?), the record businesses that distribute negative Rap, and others that push vulgar, violent, sexually charged Rap songs, videos, and personalities onto Black youth. Also, elected officials and the NAACP could sponsor some very high-profile discussions of this subject in auditoriums and on television. These discussions should be straight-out attacks on vulgar, violent, sexually charged Rap. No apologetic, compromising discussions allowed because of the *uncompromising* reality of murder, teen pregnancy, HIV/AIDS, and school failure among African American children and adolescents.

Community-Based Rites of Passage Programs

Every Black community needs a rites of passage program for our boys and girls. A rites of passage program is, generally, a one-year process composed of various teachings that, when successfully completed, transform our boys into men, and our girls into women. Black boys are taught by Black men; and Black girls are taught by Black women only. Areas covered are: definitions and examples of manhood/womanhood; the role of men/women in the family; African/African American history (never just teach African American history without first teaching African history, beginning at least 4100 B.C.); media influence on people's beliefs and behaviors; how crack cocaine, alcohol, marijuana, and other drugs impact the Black community and how alcohol and tobacco companies target youth; health issues affecting African Americans; money management; business ownership; career planning; and building healthy male-female relationships. Either we develop men and women for our communities or *White America* will!

Recommendations

The Goal

The goal of this recommendation section is multifaceted. First, we need our Black Rappers to stop assisting in the destruction of their own people. They all should be able to write chart-busting songs that do not use vulgar, sexually charged, violent lyrics; and they all should be able to make videos that do not help in sexualizing Black children and that do not whet our children's appetites for expensive material things or glamorize Blacks killing each other.

Rappers must understand that we need a redefinition of being "hard" and of being "down" that does not mean the willingness to kill, smoke weed, or have sex. If Snoop Dogg cannot make a song or a video that enhances the lives of Black girls and boys, then he must reexamine his artistic ability and whether or not he is really an artist. Can 50 Cent make songs and videos that do not contain violence, vulgarity, or strong sexual messages? If not, he, too, should reexamine his artistic ability.

The second facet of the recommendations' goal is to help our children understand, *really* understand, how influential Rappers are on the beliefs, values, and behaviors they form and help them avoid being programmed by negative Rap and negative Rappers. The third facet of the recommendations' goal is to stop recording studios, radio stations, and television stations from producing/recording/playing/showing vulgar, violent, sexually charged Rap/Rappers/videos.

111

The final recommendation is the Nguzo Saba, the seven principles. Every Black family, regardless of religion or politics, should learn and then teach and live by the Nguzo Saba. It serves as a life-enhancing guide. Maybe some of our conscientious Rappers can put a positive piece together for our kids using the Nguzo Saba.

Brothers, Sisters, and those genuinely concerned others, I hope that this writing is helpful and useful in saving the minds and, thereby, the lives of African American children residing in our African Village. Peace and Blessings.

NGUZO SABA
(The Seven Principles)

Umoja (Unity): To strive for and maintain unity in the family, community, nation, and race.

Kujichagulia (Self-Determination): To define ourselves, name ourselves, create for ourselves, and speak for ourselves instead of being defined, named, created for, and spoken for by others.

Ujima (Collective Work and Responsibility): To build and maintain our community together, and make our Sister's and Brother's problems our problems and solve them together.

Ujamma (Cooperative Economics): To build and maintain our own stores, shops, and other businesses and profit from them together.

Nia (Purpose): To make our collective vocation the building and developing of our community in order to restore our people to their traditional greatness.

Kuumba (Creativity): To do always as much as we can, in the way we can, to leave our community more beautiful and beneficial than we inherited it.

Imani (Faith): To believe with all our heart in our people, our parents, our teachers, our leaders, and the righteousness and victory of our struggle.

END NOTES

Introduction

Kunjufu, Jawanza. *Hip-Hop vs. MAAT: A Psycho/ Social Analysis of Values*. Chicago: African American Images, 1993.

Wilson, Amos N. *The Falsification of Afrikan Consciousness: Eurocentric History, Psychiatry and the Politics of White Supremacy.* Brooklyn, NY: Afrikan World Infosystems, 1993.

The Hijacking of Children's Sexual Development

Welsing, Cress Frances. *The Isis Papers: The Keys to the Colors.* Chicago: Third World Press, 1991.

Harvard Mental Health Letter, July 2005. Volume 22, Number 1. "The Adolescent Brain: Beyond Raging Hormones."

NYU Child Study Center, November 26, 2005. AboutOurKids.org.

"Toward a Better Understanding of Children's Sexual Behavior." http://www.aboutourkids.org/ aboutour/articles/sexual.html

Ryan, G. and Lane, S. *Juvenile Sexual Offending: Causes, Consequences, and Correction.* San Francisco: Jossey-Bass, 1997.

Does BET Stand for "Black Eroticizing Television"?

Center for Disease Control. *MMWR Weekly,* February 10, 2006, pp. 121-125. "Racial/Ethnic Disparities in Diagnosis of HIV/AIDS—33 States, 2001-2004."

Tweening

Schor, Juliet. *Born to Buy: The Commercialized Child and the New Consumer Culture.* New York: Scribner, 2004.

Washingtonpost.com. September 12, 2004, p. B04. Juliet Schor, "Those Ads Are Enough to Make Your Kids Sick." http://www.washington post.com/wp-dyn/articles/A13374-2004Sep11.html

Sexualized America

NYU Child Study Center. November 26, 2005. AboutOurKids.org. "Toward a Better Understanding of Children's Sexual Behavior." http://www.aboutourkids.org/aboutour/articles/sexual.html

End Notes

Paul, P. *How Pornography Is Transforming Our Lives, Our Relationships, and Our Families.* New York: New York Times Books, Henry Holt and Company. 2005.

When Pathology Becomes a Norm: Hip-Hopping into Madness

Kitwana, Bakari. *The Hip-Hop Generation.* New York: Basic Civitas Books, 2002.

Player or Sexual Predator?

Ryan, G. and Lane, S. *Juvenile Sexual Offending: Causes, Consequences, and Correction.* San Francisco: Jossey-Bass, 1997.

How Rappers Are Being Pimped

Schor, Juliet. *Born to Buy: The Commercialized Child and the New Consumer Culture.* New York: Scribner, 2004.

Where Y'all At?: Positive Rappers Search for a Black Audience

Kelley, Norman. Summer 1999. "The Political Economy of Black Music." http://www.hartford-hwp.com/archives/45a/358.html

Kunjufu, Jawanza. *Hip-Hop Street Curriculum: Keeping It Real*. Chicago: African American Images, 2005.

The Village Voice. June 24, 2005. Bakari Kitwana, "The Cotton Club: Black-Conscious Hip-Hop Deals with an Overwhelmingly White Live Audience." http://www.villagevoice.com/music/0526,kitwana,65332,22.html

Recommendations

Kunjufu, Jawanza. *Hip-Hop Street Curriculum: Keeping It Real*. Chicago: African American Images, 2005.